GREAT MOMENTS IN CRICKET

ANDREW THOMAS
and
NORMAN HARRIS

QUEEN ANNE PRESS

© Queen Anne Press Limited 1976

Among the many sources consulted, for the chapters which we contributed to this book, the following works were invaluable: John Arlott's *Alletson's Innings*, R. T. Brittenden's *Silver Fern on the Veld*, and Jack Fingleton's *The Greatest Test of All*.
– Norman Harris; Christopher Martin-Jenkins' *Testing Time*, R. E. S. Wyatt's *Three Straight Sticks*, David Frith's *My Dear Victorious Sod*, Frank Tyson's *A Typhoon called Tyson*, P. F. Warner's *How We Recovered the Ashes*, and *The Cricketer*
– Andrew Thomas.

This book is sold subject to the conditions that it shall not, by way of trade or otherwise, be lent, re-sold, hired out, or otherwise circulated without the publisher's prior consent in any form of binding or cover other than that in which it is published and without a similar condition being imposed on the subsequent purchaser.

Published by The Queen Anne Press Limited,
12 Vandy Street, London EC2A 2EN

Typeset in Plantin and printed in Great Britain by Hazell Watson & Viney Ltd, Aylesbury, Bucks

CONTENTS

From Hell to Heaven and back   5
West Indies v England, Kingston, February 1974

Day of a lifetime   11
Sussex v Nottinghamshire, Hove, May 1911

England 52, Bradman 0   16
England v Australia, The Oval, August 1948

Tennyson's men   22
Warwickshire v Hampshire, Birmingham, June 1922

Barnes-storming at Melbourne   28
Australia v England, Melbourne, December 1911

Day of distress   34
South Africa v New Zealand, Johannesburg, December 1953

Well, I declare   40
West Indies v England, Bridgetown, January 1935

Laker's Test   46
England v Australia, Manchester, July 1956

The 'impossible' victory   54
Australia v England, Sydney, December 1894

The closest Test   62
Australia v West Indies, Brisbane, December 1960

A little hatred helps   69
Australia v England, Sydney, December 1954

Everyone's Test   80
England v West Indies, Lord's, June 1963

Two for the gods   90
Australia v England, Sydney, December 1903

The last half hour   97
England v Australia, The Oval, August 1968

Napper's private wars   103
Australia v England, Sydney, December 1932
South Africa v Australia, Johannesburg, December 1935
England v Australia, Nottingham, July 1938

Indian summer   110
England v India, The Oval, August 1971

Mountains and molehills   117
Victoria v New South Wales, December 1926

G.M.T.   122
Northamptonshire v The New Zealanders, Northampton, May 1973

Cometh the hour   128
South Africa v England, Durban, December 1948

The longest day   135
West Indies v Australia, World Cup Final, Lord's, 21 June 1975

FROM HELL TO HEAVEN AND BACK

West Indies v England, Kingston, February 1974

There have not been many more curious cricket careers than that of Dennis Amiss, pride of Birmingham for almost half his life and pride of England during 1973 and 1974, when runs flowed from his bat as steadily as ticks from a clock. His great run began in Pakistan early in 1973, when he rose from a sick-bed to score 112 at Lahore. He followed this with 158 at Hyderabad, and seemed certain to make a hat trick of hundreds in the three Test matches when Sarfraz caught him at short-leg off Intikhab for 99 at Karachi.

At home, against New Zealand, he held his form, scoring a century in the first Test, a half-century in the second, and finishing second to Geoff Boycott in the averages. Then came West Indies for the second half of the 1973 summer, and against this stiffer opposition Amiss was held to a top score of 86 not out and a relatively modest average of 46. That, thought some folk, was the end of a pretty little sequence. So heavily had England been beaten by West Indies that Englishmen everywhere felt foreboding as they contemplated the winter series in the Caribbean, where Rohan Kanhai's West Indians would probably be even more invincible on their own fast pitches.

As if the prospects weren't grim enough, England had shelved her previously successful leader Ray Illingworth and, midst widespread misgivings and shaking of heads, appointed Scottish-born Mike Denness as captain. The first Test, at Port-of-Spain, was lost by seven wickets, though Amiss hung on in the second innings for 174 in over six and a half hours and posted 209 for the first wicket with Boycott. It was a feast day for pessimists. Would England lose all five Tests?

By the fourth evening of the second Test – at Sabina Park, Kingston, Jamaica – it seemed they were well on their way.

Winning the toss, Denness had claimed first use of a batsman's pitch, but the opportunity of raising a large score was tossed away by England with some careless strokes. The fast bowling of Boyce, Julien, and Sobers and the leg-spin of Barrett and off-spin of Gibbs compelled close attention but beset the batsmen with no insurmountable problems. The West Indian fielding was, as usual, keen and supple, and the catches that England offered up with sickening frequency were gathered in gleefully. Only a fifth-wicket stand of 90 between Denness, the captain, and Tony Greig, his vice-captain, ensured anything but a dismal total. As it was, the 353 obtained just after lunch on the second day was dwarfed by a West Indian total of 583 for 9 declared – Lawrence Rowe 120, Roy Fredericks 94, Alvin Kallicharran 93, Bernard Julien 66, Garry Sobers 57, Clive Lloyd 49 – a sort of Caribbean charity gala.

Facing arrears of 230, with almost 10 hours of the match remaining, England suffered a bruising blow to morale when Boycott, fending at a nasty short ball from Boyce, was caught at the wicket for five. England 32 for one.

John Jameson, Amiss's burly Warwickshire team-mate, came in, a fearless and willing hooker of the bouncer. There could be only one kind of greeting, and Boyce leapt in and released it: a vicious bouncer at Jameson's eyes. He hooked compulsively, and the ball flew off the top edge of the bat for six over third man! His second ball had to be a bouncer too, and this time he hooked with more certainty and gained four runs. He went on to 38, taking the total to 102, before Kanhai – who also happened to be a Warwickshire player – secured his wicket through Barrett, the leg-spinner. Kanhai was as aware as any man that Jameson was seldom comfortable against spin.

So that was another England batsman wheedled out: eight more needed. Next in was young Lancastrian Frank Hayes, who had scored 106 not out against West Indies at The Oval in his first Test match, seven months before. He had faltered since that heartening beginning, but English hope still rested heavily upon his golden head. Here was a chance for him to bat and bat and bat . . . until his side was safe and his own bright promise and reputation restored. Before Hayes had scored, Amiss tapped a ball to cover and called for a quick single. Clive Lloyd, the world's greatest cover fielder, scooped up the ball and flung it towards the stumps with his customary accuracy. Hayes was beaten narrowly. England 107 for 3, Amiss past his 50 but utterly crestfallen.

Denness came in and again there was dogged resistance. A

high wind may have blown down part of the Sabina Park scoreboard carrying the names of England's batsmen, yet the tourists continued to disregard the incident – or any other – as an augury. The total was lifted to 176, and the clock hands had moved slowly round, before Denness, to the surprise of himself and several others, was adjudged caught by Rowe at slip off an apparent 'bat-and-pad'. England 217 for 4, with more than a day to go, the sky so blue it might never have held rain and would probably never see it in months to come.

The extremely tall, lean, and blond-haired Tony Greig strode out to join Amiss now, a refreshingly combative cricketer, South African-born, extrovert, and to be England's captain a year hence when the selectors brought Mike Denness's mixed reign to an end. Greig's arrival at the crease gave the tiring Amiss new heart. With a square cut off Sobers he reached his century, and as the next ball was a full toss he clubbed it for six in celebration. Then it was back to the depressing task of preventing wickets from falling, willing the clock to move on over 24 hours. The salt tablets continued to do their job through his thick and fatigued limbs.

The candle-flame of hope flickered wildly again that evening as Greig, having made 14, was bowled as he pushed forward to off-spinner Gibbs. Derek Underwood, England's loyal nightwatchman, came in with a quarter of an hour remaining, to spare Alan Knott, the last partner for Amiss of whom anything could be realistically expected. 'Unders' survived, one not out, and England went to bed at 218 for 5, still 12 runs behind with one whole day remaining. Dennis Amiss was 123 not out.

A new ball was available first thing on that last morning, but Kanhai chose to give his spinners a few overs at the start. It could have decided the match, for the third ball, from Gibbs, spun across Amiss's bat and flew to short-leg, where Sobers, who had become the first man to reach 8000 runs in Tests during West Indies' innings, put his name on the obverse side of the match by missing this sharp chance. The fielding side were naturally annoyed, as were the local spectators, who watched for the kill from all sorts of vantage points. But another chance would come. It was bound to.

But England's cricketers this day were to prove very obstinate. Underwood played resolutely forward with steeply-angled bat as if, according to BBC broadcaster Chris Martin-Jenkins, he were 'a suspicious bomb disposal officer'.

Soon the innings defeat was averted. Boyce, West Indies'

most hostile bowler, crashed the ball into the blameless wicket but failed to disturb either tailender or opener. The sixth wicket added 41 runs and – more importantly – stretched through an hour and a half. Underwood had served gallantly for his side when Sobers had him caught by Murray at the wicket for 12. Knott, the last recognised batsman, emerged.

Amiss had initiated some smartly stolen runs between his authoritative boundary shots, but when Knott had made but six, Amiss played a ball to cover, Lloyd, and set off for a run. Lloyd's throw knocked the middle stump out with Knott still stretching for safety. It was an eerie repetition of the Hayes tragedy the day before, just as bitter for its being uncalled for in the circumstances, just as unsettling for the eternal Amiss, who had to accept total blame and yet remain unwavering in his duty to see England through, unlikely though this now seemed.

This brought in Chris Old, the Yorkshire fast bowler and hard-hitting left-hand batsman. If he had a problem at all it was to restrain himself. He was never happier than when thrashing the bowling; yet the equation that began to matter was England's lead against the time remaining. From now on runs counted virtually double. The deficit was behind England. Every run now had to be made also by West Indies if they were to win.

Old kept Amiss company until lunchtime, when England were 64 ahead with the solid, grimacing Amiss 162 not out.

Arthur Barrett, the accurate and persistent Jamaican leg-spinner, eventually prised out Old as he tried to drive him. His 19 had occupied a precious 110 minutes during which Kanhai had tried everything on him, even some Boyce bouncers. Now it was the turn of Pat 'Percy' Pocock, the Surrey off-spinner, to hold an end up. He had done so conspicuously well several times in past Test matches, but his early overs gave frights galore to his team-mates and the pink-faced English supporters in the stand, as he aimed airy drives at Barrett. Then he seemed to remember his mission, and began playing the long defensive stretch forward which Underwood had employed so admirably that morning.

At last Dennis Amiss, having passed his previous highest score of 192, enjoyed the new and rare experience of reaching 200, brought with a cover-drive to the boundary off Sobers. The statistical significance penetrated his growing numbness, but he departed not for a moment from his Herculean determination to 'just keep on batting'. He knew the umpires would lift the bails when the ordeal was over, and that he would be led to the pavilion. There could be only one awareness: that the West Indies must be defied. Risks must be shunned for a couple more hours, and the strike must be retained to protect the tail-enders whenever possible – without adding a further tragic run-out.

At tea England were 145 ahead, and one hour plus 20 overs remained. If the last two wickets fell swiftly West Indies would have a strong chance to go two-up with three to play. Yet so dispirited were the home side that they were three or four minutes late returning to the field after tea. Amiss and his blocking partners had almost won the day already.

It was just after four o'clock when Pocock was caught at cover, and the long, raw-boned figure of fast bowler Bob Willis, the last man in, took over the shift. He proved immovable, and as Amiss passed 250, and listeners in Britain picked up the astounding news on radio, a euphoria of relief and exultation spread across all who love a brave marathon.

When England were out of reach, the match was called off, with half an hour's possible playing time left. Willis was 3 not out, England were 432 for 9, and Amiss, the name on every-one's lips, was 262 not out, having been deprived of the honour of 'carrying his bat' when Willis remained undefeated. Amiss had hit a six and 40 fours, and in nine and a half hours he had consumed countless salt tablets and a good deal of liquid, re-duced the eager crowd almost to silence, registered the eighth-highest score ever for England in Test cricket, and displayed technical skills and an iron will that enabled a disillusioned British sporting public to hold its head high in pride once more.

Fletcher, Greig, and Knott made enough runs to save Eng-land in the third Test, and in the fourth, in Guyana, Amiss made his third century of the series. Greig made another, and though rain ruined the match it was becoming apparent that England were now a much harder side to beat. By the fifth Test, back at Port-of-Spain, they were a positive danger, Boy-cott making 99, then Greig, with his newly-found off-spinners, taking 8 for 86. A second-innings Boycott century left West Indies needing 226 for victory. Greig took another five wickets and Underwood secured the vital wicket of Sobers, and Eng-land pulled off a sensational victory by 26 runs to level the series one-all. It took some digesting. And it all began with Amiss's epic at Kingston.

He went on scoring runs in England in the summer that followed, making 188 against India and 183 against Pakistan, and by the time he flew off to Australia in October 1974 he had piled up 2140 runs, with eight centuries, in 35 Test innings (five of them not-out) since March 1973, at an average of 71.3. This mountain had been built attractively and at a steady rate, and Amiss eventually took over Boycott's mantle as England's finest batsman. The ghastly memory of Amiss's first Test match against Australia, in 1968 at Old Trafford, when he scored 0 and 0, had shrunk from nightmare to wry joke.

Yet heartbreak was round the corner. In Australia during the 1974-75 series his technique was found lacking against the raw pace of Dennis Lillee and Jeff Thomson. He was out of luck, too – something no sportsman can do without. He suffered a broken thumb in being struck by a ball from Thomson at Brisbane, and missed the second Test. In the third, at Melbourne, he needed 97 runs to pass Bobby Simpson's world Test record of 1381 runs in a calendar year. Amiss made only four of them in the first innings, but advanced to 90 in the second – three more required – when, having lost his early impetus and suffering from his old enemy, cramp, he spooned a Mallett off-break to mid-wicket and was caught.

It was not just a fatal falter at the last hurdle; it was the end of the good times. He made 12 and 37 in the next Test, when England lost the Ashes, and 0 and 0 in the next – return of the nightmare. In the final Test his misfortunes continued: he batted once and again failed to score, dismissed by Lillee.

He had two Test innings in New Zealand, and one of them was 164 not out, but back in England he faced the Australians again and his ignominy was complete with 4, 5, 0, and 10 before the selectors had no option but to drop him. The fast bowlers, chiefly Lillee, had got him each time. What a reversal: 2140 runs in 35 Test innings, then 194 in 13 innings against Australia!

Dennis Amiss may return to the England XI to add to this curious pattern of outrageous success and pathetic failure. Whether he does or not, his purple patch will be talked about as long as people discuss cricket. And the greatest innings of a most distinguished sequence will remain his death-defying 262 not out at Kingston, when an hour after the match he was calmly and unaffectedly puffing at his pipe. Indeed, several weeks later he was still writing to admirers thanking them for the trouble they took in sending him telegrams of congratulation. Here was a man who had known both Heaven and Hell.

A. T.

DAY OF A LIFETIME

Sussex v Nottinghamshire, Hove, May 1911

A photograph of Edwin Boaler Alletson might almost, but for his cricket attire, be titled: 'Ted Alletson, the Nottinghamshire prize fighter'. The features are also, of course, comparatively youthful, and unmarked. But one recognises the simple calm of a man who *knows* his strength; and one sees, too, the powerful head and neck, the broad shoulders and full chest and, especially, the long, muscular forearms. In fact his arm span was almost six inches greater than his height. He moved, in the words of one contemporary, 'with the springy tread of the Zulus'.

Obviously, here was a man capable of hard hitting – and also, perhaps, of quick bowling. It was mainly as a bowler that, at the age of 14, he played among men for the Welbeck estate of the Duke of Portland (on which estate his father was a wheelright), though at the age of 20 it was with a vigorous innings for the estate team against bowling, which included the county stalwart Hallam, that he was invited to join the ground staff at Trent Bridge.

His progress, however, was not dramatic. His bowling – which may well have been his main strength, if developed – was given scant opportunity throughout his career with Notts. He remained one of those batsmen who bat amongst the all-rounders at six, seven, or eight, but without bowling enough to be a fully-fledged all-rounder. In 1906 he played only three innings, for two runs. In 1907, his first full season, he had a top score of 40. By 1911 his top score was 81; in the previous season he had scored a few half-centuries, but his average over all that summer was still no better than 20. It was said that the Duke of Portland had promised him a cheque for £100 when he made his first century for the county; if this were so, at least the handsome prize had not yet been claimed. He had made his runs, when he got them, rather briskly – without ever batting long enough to seriously alarm the opposition. He played straight, and tended to either block or hit straight.

One of the sides he had made some quick runs against in that previous summer was Sussex. Now, for the second game of the 1911 season, Nottinghamshire again travelled south to Hove. This time – as on some other occasions – Ted Alletson was not sure of his place in the XI. Two men had injuries, and he was one of them, being troubled by a wrist strain. In the event it was decided that his injury was the one that would be least aggravated by playing. The previous season he had at one point risen to six in the batting order; now he was nine.

Notts won the toss and batted first. A. O. Jones, captain and opening batsman, made sound runs, and George Gunn was stumped 10 short of a century; Notts were within reach of 200 with only three wickets down, but were then bowled out for 238 by the left-arm 'occasional' bowling of Killick, who got 5 for 14. Ted Alletson was out for seven. Sussex spent the remainder of the first day and the best part of the second establishing a commanding lead. When Notts went in again they had to get 177 to make Sussex bat again. This time Jones was out straightaway but his partner Iremonger settled in. On the third morning Iremonger and George Gunn were beginning to make free with the bowling when, at 129, Gunn – again – was stumped. Before long, Hardstaff, John Gunn, Payton, Whysall, and Iremonger were out; Notts were 185 for 7, only nine runs on, and Alletson was in.

He came to the wicket with his own special bat, very light at two pounds three ounces, but with a handle thickened by the addition of an extra rubber sleeve; and hoping that his wrist, following a dip in the sea that morning, might not trouble him too much. His partner was Lee, another all-rounder in name if not always in practice. The bowlers were the Relf brothers, Robert the slow bowler and the vastly experienced, immaculately accurate Albert with his testing medium-pace and movement off the wicket. Alletson made a bright start, going to double figures in five minutes. Lee went with him. Two hundred on the board became 230. Some 25 minutes before lunch, Robert Relf was replaced by the opening bowler Leach and then Albert Relf by Killick, who bowled left-arm medium-pace.

In Killick's first over, Alletson pushed up the line as usual and got an edge which flew low and awkwardly to slip, to the left hand of Cox, who could not hold it. Alletson was 42. But almost immediately Cox held another chance off Leach, to send back Lee. In Leach's next over, he bowled the new batsman, wicket-keeper Oates; and, without last batsman Riley coming in, lunch was taken with Notts 260 for 9. Alletson, having added 73 in 40 minutes with Lee for the eighth wicket, was himself 48 at lunch. For him, this was as brisk as he customarily scored. What followed was far to exceed it and, in the course of no more than three-quarters of an hour, to make the number nine batsman famous.

During the interval, Alletson was heard to ask his captain if, with one wicket left and only 84 runs on, it really mattered how he now played. A. O. Jones said he thought not. In that case, said Alletson, he was going to go for Tim Killick.

Resuming after lunch at 2.20 p.m., the remainder of Leach's over was first completed. Number 11 Riley survived the four balls. Then Alletson faced Killick. He took fours from the second and third balls, then a single. Riley had only two balls to play, but got a single off the second. Retaining the strike was *not* his function, and to the first ball of the next over, against Leach, he smartly took a single. For the first time after lunch, Alletson faced Leach, a bowler off whom he had taken runs the previous year at Brighton, but who had since moved up a couple of notches from change bowler to brisk opener. Now Alletson struck him firmly for two, four, and two off consecutive balls, and then a single from the last ball.

He was now well warmed up, ready for Killick's new over, and he had the left-armer's line now. Beyond the bowler, the field ran away down to the beckoning southern stand. The first ball he drove straight for six, likewise the last ball, and in between took two fours and a two. Twenty-two off the over, and the score had jumped past 300.

Leach bowled to Riley, and Riley, splendid fellow, got the second ball away and ran furiously for a three to relinquish the strike. Alletson now swung straight into the quicker bowler. He planted him too, for six, and four, and ended the over by nicking one from which they ran another three, giving Alletson the strike – and his 100.

A welcome pause at the end of the over, and he faced Killick again. Eleven more came off this over, and then Leach. Another six, two fours, and a three. If the ball was up to the bat, he drove it flat; if not, he hit under it and lifted it straight. If it was very short he 'snipped' it away square to off or on. Off the fifth ball of each of these overs, Alletson got to the other end and Riley blocked the sixth.

For the bespectacled Tim Killick, a man of artistic tastes and gentle good humour, bowling had become unpleasant and genuinely frightening. In this next over he twice no-balled, evidently in his anxiety to avoid being hit by the returning ball. The ball when struck, low like a shell, was humming through the air. Even fieldsmen on the fence were in danger if actually getting their hands to one. Alletson, standing up straight, drove again and again, driving harder than Jessop: clean, ringing strokes. And from the back foot the ball whistled square to the main pavilion, one smashing the clock, another breaking a window and damaging the bar. At the end of this over by poor Tim Killick the scoreboard had spun frantically on from 346 to 380 – 34 in the eight-ball over, with four, six, six, nought, four, four, four, six. (A record for first-class cricket, until Garry Sobers surpassed it with his six sixes, in 1968.)

The Hove crowd had been cheering madly throughout. Memories would expand with years, so that more balls were lost out of the ground than actually were hit for sixes, and one ball would be earnestly said to have been so propelled as to embed itself in the soft wood of the pavilion, needing a chisel to extract it. But the actual statistics were even more astonishing. In the course of just five consecutive overs – three from Killick and two from Leach – Alletson had scored 97 runs out of 100. The admirable Riley had in these five overs contrived to play just four balls.

Now Sussex were forced to make a double bowling change. Against two of the shrewdest county professionals, Albert Relf and George Cox (senior), Alletson took a few balls to start picking up the new line, and at the other end Riley found more difficulty in taking the single. So, two overs produced but eight runs. Then Alletson was away again on a final charge. He hit Relf for six, taking 15 off the over, and getting a single off the last ball. Against Cox, he thumped the first two balls for four, ignored a single off the third (as he had done, in the middle of any over, since lunch) and then lofted him high and straight. After so many balls had passed beyond the reach of relieved fieldsmen, this time a man was under it. C. L. A. Smith, the Sussex acting captain, held the ball securely, though he was (as even a Hove newspaper reported) 'standing against the grandstand'. Nottinghamshire players saw it too; but Alletson, happily walking off to tumultuous applause, was not concerned. With 189 to his name, he had had enough, and Notts now needed the time to try and bowl Sussex out.

They almost did, too, Sussex in the end drawing the game

at 213 for 8. More remarkable than the result, or the near-result, was the time span in which the opportunity was fashioned: Notts had resumed after lunch at 20 minutes past two, 84 runs on, and at around three o'clock finished their innings leaving Sussex a target of 237. In that brief post-lunch period of some 40 minutes, the tenth wicket had added 152, Alletson making 142 of them.

In his next innings, a few days later at Bristol, he went in and scored 60 in the last half-hour of the day; and two years later he played some rapid innings of which the best was 88 out of 109 in 40 minutes, while in another he hit Wilfred Rhodes for three consecutive sixes. But he never quite achieved the same prolonged devastation as on his day of days at Hove. It was said that he lost his hitting capability by trying to improve his defence. His captain A. O. Jones told of the frustration of guaranteeing him a place as a hitter, no matter how many failures he might make, so long as he *did hit* – but he would not do it. He played in a Test trial, but scored few runs. That apart, all the first-class cricket he played was for Notts, and in a career spanning seven full seasons and 179 innings he made just the one, utterly memorable, century.

One of the several witnesses to that innings, John Gunn, has said (in *Alletson's Innings* by John Arlott): 'He was a good chap, Ted, and a real trier; you would not call him a great player, but once or twice a season he would hit harder than anyone else I have even seen.'

N. H.

ENGLAND 52, BRADMAN 0

England v Australia, The Oval, August 1948

The England v Australia Test match at The Oval in 1948 contained two dramatic events which, in truth, were unconnected, even though they were embraced within the same scoresheet. They deserved to have been featured separately. Instead, Bradman's last Test innings and England's lowest-ever total in England (their second-lowest anywhere) exist side by side, to be spoken of still with sadness or ghoulish delight.

Saturday, 14 August 1948 saw the complete enactment. Norman Yardley, winning the toss for England, took first innings on a pitch that had been saturated by rain during the week and overnight. His decision, of course, was much more roundly criticised later, when England had been torpedoed with hardly any trace. His considerations as to treacherous footholds for the bowlers, a probably sluggish wicket until it firmed up, and the nuisance of a slippery ball for fast and slower bowlers alike came to nothing. The innings became a procession as batsmen made their way to the middle, scattered as it was with sawdust, and dragged their dismal way back to the shelter of the dressing-room.

The series, the first against Australia in England since the war, had been lop-sided, though England had had the better of the third Test, at Old Trafford, when rain spoilt the final stages. Then they had played very respectably at Leeds until the final day, when Australia made an unprecedented – and since unequalled – 404 to win by seven wickets. Denis Compton, England's leading hero, scored a stirring 184 at Trent Bridge and 145, interrupted by a gashed eyebrow when he mis-hit Lindwall, at Old Trafford. Bill Edrich and Cyril Washbrook made centuries at Leeds, but all in all the Australian fast attack of Lindwall, Miller, and Johnston, assisted by the regulation that a new ball could be taken after only 55 overs, had carried all before it. For the only time in his 20-year career in Test cricket, Len Hutton was dropped, such was England's confusion and depression. His replacement, Emmett of Gloucestershire, failed, and Yorkshire's pale and slim champion was restored to the England side and, if anything, showed the benefit of his rehabilitation by scoring 81 and 57 in the fourth Test. And now, here at The Oval, he was to demonstrate yet again how he was really in a class of his own.

Hutton took with him to open the innings not Washbrook, his regular partner, but John Dewes, 21, of Cambridge University. Dewes had made 40 for the University and 51 for Middlesex against the touring team, and was highly thought of; it was, nevertheless, considered by most people who cared that his baptism in Test cricket was entirely premature. Whether the more experienced Washbrook, out with a badly damaged thumb, would have saved England from the forthcoming indignity is doubtful.

The start of play was delayed half an hour by the damp conditions, and at midday, with humidity high, Lindwall, with his beautiful flowing action, began the attack from the Vauxhall end. The batsmen took a single each from the over (Dewes's obvious nervousness communicating itself to all who watched), and then the tall, dark-haired, loose-limbed Miller took up the bowling with the pavilion behind him. To his second ball, Dewes stretched forward hopefully and was bowled middle-stump.

Edrich, a small, pugnacious figure, came in to affectionate applause – a proven saviour of his side on countless occasions. The pitch, in this short time, had displayed no sign of undue viciousness; nor did Bradman's field placing suggest there was any devil in it. After three overs from Miller, he was replaced by Bill Johnston, the balding, gangling, left-arm medium-pacer from Victoria.

In 20 minutes Edrich managed three runs, and England were just into double figures. Johnston dropped one short just outside leg-stump, and Edrich launched into one of his favourite shots, the hook. It sent the ball backward of square-leg, where the small hands of Hassett clasped it as the fieldsman completed an agile dive. The little Victorian was soon drawing more applause – this time for chivalry – as Compton, looking shaky against Lindwall, popped a ball from that bowler high over the slips and dropped his bat. Hutton called for a run, but the striker suffered a mental blockage. With one eye on Hassett, running in from third man, and the other flitting between his grounded bat and his batting partner, he took off for the run so late that Hutton was already at the striker's end. As Compton fled desperately for safety at the far end, Hassett, smiling, chivalrously held the ball.

It made little difference to the grim course of England's innings. Compton, the gay cavalier, the 'Brylcreem boy', idol of every cricket-loving and football-loving lad in London and many other places, was soon facing Ray Lindwall again, and hooking at a short ball – rather late – only to put it straight to Morris at square-leg. The fieldsman was sited precisely there by Bradman, who recalled Compton's placement of the shot in previous years. England 17 for 3, and thoughts now turning away from estimates of what would be a secure total to whether humiliation was to be avoided.

Jack Crapp, Gloucestershire's Cornish left-hander, entered, and six runs were squeezed in 20 minutes – none of them to him. Miller replaced Lindwall, and mesmerised Crapp with a lifter which he touched to wicket-keeper Tallon. England 23 for 4. Miller three wickets for two runs off six overs. In came the captain, Yardley, with every opportunity to play a skipper's knock worthy of Tennysonian tribute. He, at least, survived until lunch, taken at 29 for 4 after a torrid 90 minutes' play. The classical Hutton, who had never been seriously inconvenienced, was 17, Yardley 4.

As the lunch interval approached, Bradman had begun to draw his field in closer to the bat, and one ball from Johnston rapped Hutton sharply on the glove as he played defensively forward with his immaculately straight bat. There was growing evidence that things, far from improving, could only get worse.

Ray Lindwall, 26, the fair-haired New South Welshman who had struck fear into the hearts of batsmen all over England on this the first of his three tours, returned to the attack after lunch, and bowled Yardley with a very fast ball of full length which kept a shade low: 35 for 5, last man 7. Yardley's was to be the second-highest score of the innings.

Allan Watkins, the third left-hander, was a surprise choice for this match. He had hooked the Australian fast bowlers with a degree of confidence while batting for Glamorgan, and with his medium-pace left-arm bowling and brilliant short-leg fielding he was expected to contribute appreciably as a genuine all-rounder. The selection of him and the other newcomers brought England's total of players used during the 1948 series to 22 – an unhappy near-comparison with the 1921 series, when Australia destroyed chiefly through the fast pair Gregory and McDonald.

Watkins, the first Welshman to play against Australia, was soon taking physical punishment when a flyer from Lindwall penetrated an unavailing flat-bat hook stroke and struck him on the point of the left shoulder. The blow was to render him ineffective as a bowler later in the match.

Soon he was hit on the pad by Johnston and the umpire's finger was raised in answer to the lusty appeal. England now 42 for 6, and as usual in these situations as news spread round the city more and more people rushed to the ground to experience the sensations.

Who was next? Partisans wished it could have been a second Hutton, for the frail Yorkshireman, who had scored 364 in England's 903 for 7 on this ground 10 years earlier, was still there, as seemingly immovable as his colleagues were ephemeral. In came the jaunty Godfrey Evans, wicket-keeper and lively batsman and runner-between-wickets. He made one run then Lindwall bowled him as he played helplessly forward.

Alec Bedser came in, England's lionhearted opening bowler. He had a brand new bat, and as he departed moments later, bowled by Lindwall for 0, the blade still had that virgin look about it.

That made it 45 for 8, and one run was needed to overtake England's lowest ever in Test cricket, 45 against Australia at Sydney in the 1886–87 series. Jack Young, the Middlesex slow left-arm bowler, joined Hutton, and the score reached 47 before he too was bowled by Lindwall for a duck. Lindwall was showing what he had first shown in the 1946–47 series: that he was a skilful mopper-up of tailenders. His outlook towards them was also recalled nearly 30 years later when Lillee and Thomson were bowling bouncers at late-order batsmen: Lindwall always felt that if he couldn't bowl out numbers 9, 10, and 11 without resorting to intimidation then he ought not to be wearing Australia's colours as a fast bowler.

The last man in was Eric Hollies, a considerable leg-spin bowler but quite incompetent batsman. Hutton got the bowling, hit the only boundary of the innings when he lofted Lindwall far and straight. And then, when it seemed certain he would become only the second England batsman to carry his bat through a complete innings against Australia (an honour he was eventually to chalk up at Adelaide two and a half years later) he glanced Lindwall – a good-looking shot, a typical Hutton shot – but through the air, and Don Tallon, the tall wicket-keeper, hurled himself to his left and scooped up a grand one-handed catch.

England all out 52. That was something to stop homeward-bound schoolboys and businessmen in their tracks. Hutton had made 30 of them, in two and a half hours, and Lindwall's figures were 16.1 overs, five maidens, six wickets for 20. Since lunch he had taken 5 for 8 off 8.1 overs. 'The world', he later wrote, 'looked very rosy.'

Lindwall felt that England's batsmen had been too distrustful of the pitch, expecting the ball to fly from a length. 'Actually it went through at uniform height. At least four were bowled by yorkers.' He was inspired as much as anything by the return to his crouching, menacing position at short-leg of Sid Barnes, who had taken a sickening blow in the kidney while fielding in the 'suicide' position in the Manchester Test.

Barnes now came out with Morris to start Australia's innings, and in an hour England's total was passed. In another hour the score had reached 117 when Hollies spun a leg-break across the face of Barnes's bat and Evans took the catch, standing over the stumps. There had been only one semblance of a chance in the partnership before that, when Young had failed to hold a hard, low hit at point by Barnes off Bedser.

This brought in Don Bradman, and with him the expectation of a gigantic score. He was 13 days from his 40th birthday, and four months from a knighthood. This was his last Test match – pretty obviously his final Test innings, considering the state of the game. He had been dismissed 69 times while scored 6996 runs in his uniquely glorious 20-year career, and therefore needed a mere four runs to be sure of a Test career average of 100. In his 79 innings to date in Test cricket he had notched 29 centuries, 19 of them off England bowling. These were both easily record figures. Indeed, the man's name had been garlanded with batting records of all kinds. His surname was a synonym for superiority. It had stood for a legend since before some of the younger members of the audience this day had been born. And now it was all drawing to a close. Having fought off several illnesses, one of which had put him in serious doubt as to whether he could resume big cricket after the war, 'the Don' was now compelled to concede that age was getting its own miserable way. Most cricketers would have settled on being able to bat like Bradman even when he was in his fortieth year, but he himself had exacting standards.

Thus, as he walked slowly to the middle, where Yardley and his England team prepared to give him three rousing cheers, a long and glowing chapter in history was drawing to a close. He took guard, looked perfunctorily around the field, and settled over his bat. John Arlott's commentary on BBC radio told the tale as well as any one could demand:

'And now here's Hollies to bowl to him from the Vauxhall end. He bowls. Bradman goes back across his wicket. He pushes the ball gently in the direction of the Houses of Parliament, which are out beyond mid-off. It doesn't go that far. It merely goes to Watkins at silly mid-off. No run. Still 117 for one. Two slips, a silly mid-off, and a forward short-leg close to him, as Hollies pitches the ball up slowly and ... he's bowled! (Applause from all round the ground.) Bradman, bowled Hollies, nought, and what do you say under those circumstances?'

Much was said in the hours, days, and years that followed. Did Bradman have tears in his eyes? He never said much about it. He left the scene that Saturday evening and someone had to take his place. It was Hassett. Arthur Morris went on to make 196, but that is largely overlooked. Australia made 389, Hollies finished with five wickets, and England were bowled out again, this time for 188, Hutton top-scored once more, making 64. Australia won by an innings and 149 runs. But much of this is forgotten.

England's humiliation, Hutton's dignity, Lindwall's relentless speed and accuracy, Hollies' googly, which had no respect for statistical tidiness – these phenomena live on in the minds of those who were there and those who heard and read of the cricket at Kennington Oval on that extraordinary August Saturday in 1948.

A.T.

TENNYSON'S MEN

Warwickshire v Hampshire, Birmingham, June 1922

At the end of the first day, there would be those who found it easy to say, 'Typical Tennyson'. Typical optimism, typical gambling. Lionel, Lord Tennyson, captain of England and Hampshire and a big boy, really, in a jaunty-angled cap, had put Warwickshire in to bat and been made to look foolish. In fact, the decision may well have been sound enough. There had been enough rain just to moisten the surface, and the pitch promised to offer life at least during the morning – though it was soon to recover. Tennyson had his stalwart opening bowlers Kennedy and Newman, one an England player and the other close to it, whom often enough he bowled throughout an entire innings; and he had the lively left-arm of Boyes as first change.

Initially, the decision worked for Tennyson. Newman, cutting the ball quite nastily, got an early first wicket in the leg trap, a second with a catch at slip, and a third by hitting leg-stump. Warwickshire were then 44 for 3. It was only by vigorous counter-attack that Warwickshire improved with the young number three, Santall, partnering Calthorpe, a captain who always sought enjoyment in the cricket for himself and his side. Thinnish, angular, good-humoured, he struck three sixes. The third, off Kennedy, went over long-on, over the professionals' dressing-room, over the road, and landed about 15 yards into a field adjoining Cannon Hill Park. In all, however, Warwickshire's was an innings of just one partnership. Though Calthorpe and Santall had passed 160 in their fourth-wicket partnership, Warwickshire were all out for 223. The pitch was now playing well, but the Warwickshire batting from the middle down was poor.

Then Hampshire which began its reply at around four o'clock was one of the strongest batting sides in the country. It contained Tennyson himself, always a spirited performer; one of the greatest of all left-hand batsmen in Philip Mead; another England batsman, George Brown, at number six; and the opener Bowell, who was near to Test standard. Already this season, Mead – ridiculing his grave pneumonia of the winter – had scored 235 in 285 minutes against Yorkshire, a match that Hampshire won by an innings. And against Kent, when set 444 to win, Hampshire got past 350 for four wickets before being all out for 392 – a decent enough score in the fourth innings. Now they faced Howell, who was quick – he had gone on the last tour to Australia, and the previous season had taken exactly 100 wickets despite missing 10 games with a bad foot – and the other opening bowler was Calthorpe himself. Much depended on these two, with Partridge and Simms out of the side. Evidently they were aware of that.

Howell bowled the first over of the innings to Bowell, who played out a maiden. Calthorpe bowled the second to Kennedy, a steady opener as well as, mainly, a bowler. Off the third ball Kennedy was caught at the wicket. Howell again, to Bowell, produced a snorter, breaking the batsman's middle stump and sending the debris to the feet of the 'keeper standing back. It was as good a ball as he had ever bowled. Calthorpe, in his second over, to the young H. L. V. Day of Eton and Cambridge, bowled him sixth ball with a cruelly good delivery. Three wickets had fallen for no runs. The presence of Tennyson and Mead suggested an end of nonsense.

In Howell's third over, Mead took a single off the first ball. Then Tennyson edged a quick one, very nearly to hand, over the slips for four. He obviously knew little about it, and next ball played unhappily in the air towards mid-on, where Calthorpe flung himself forward to take a brilliant catch. Brown came in, a Test hero, and Howell clean-bowled him first ball. Five wickets down for five, but Mead increased the score dramatically when, to the first ball of Calthorpe's next over, he hooked for four. It was to be the only militant stroke of the innings. He played out the rest of the over, then Howell was let loose at the new batsman, Newman: off the second ball, caught at slip. Shirley came in to get the first ball away past point for a single but then, at the other end against Calthorpe, was caught low in the slips. In the same over, two balls later, McIntyre was given lbw. Eight wickets for 10. Howell again, permitted Mead a single, saw four byes go down the leg side, and then in consecutive balls got Livsey and Boyes, numbers 10 and 11, clean-bowled and lbw.

With Hampshire all out for 15, Howell had taken six wickets for seven and Calthorpe four for four. The chart of their nine overs reads as follows:

Howell	. .	. W	1 W	. .	1 W
	. .	. .	4 .	W .	. W
	. .	. .	W .	. 1	. .
Calthorpe	. .	. .	4 .	. W	
	. .	. .	. .	W .	
	W .	. W	. .	. .	

Hampshire, batting for only 40 minutes, had made one of the lowest scores in all first-class cricket. Indeed, it would have been a world record, but for those four byes. 'Tiger' Smith behind the stumps claimed he was unsighted. Anyway, seven batsmen made ducks, those to score being Tennyson with his streaky four, Shirley with a single, and Mead, who remained not out for six. What had happened? Was the wicket not as recovered as it appeared? Was the bowling devilishly good? Or the batting dreadfully bad?

Many were the opinions given over the years. Mead was to profess that he was baffled by it all, as 'Nobody bowled me anything that I could not play in the middle'. That rather conflicted, however, with H. L. V. Day's description of his own dismissal: 'The ball started at mid-on and finished at third slip, bowling me on the way.' And Howell, according to his own 'keeper, had bowled quite above his own standards of speed. Perhaps the best of judgments was that in the following morning's *Birmingham Post*: 'Calthorpe and Howell, realising the weakness of the attack in the absence of Partridge and Simms, opened up with rare vim and, meeting with early success, got their tails up; the batsmen, as had happened before and would happen again, had their confidence shaken to pieces; Howell forgot about movement off the pitch and went for all-out pace, while Calthorpe relied almost wholly on swing and seam; and everything worked for the home side, every possible catch was taken, and for an historic 40 minutes Warwickshire were as faultless as any cricket team was ever likely to be.'

In thousands of cricket matches it must happen that such events will transpire, almost according to the law of averages – though at the time it was a little hard for Hampshire to see it like that. Still, Tennyson was splendidly bluff. He announced to his unnerved men that they would make 500 in the follow-on. And when Calthorpe came from the Warwickshire dressing-room and genially suggested a golf match the next day between both teams' amateurs, Tennyson gave him a broadside, declaring that his men would be batting until lunchtime on the third day. *And*, he added, they would win the match. Typical

Tennyson. An amused Calthorpe staked £10 against Hampshire doing just that.

So relaxed was Calthorpe as Warwickshire took the field again that he did not immediately put Howell on, remarking that to do this might be unfair on the paying spectators. At any rate, Hampshire had made only a modest beginning – though it was exactly as many as they had totalled in the first effort – when at 15 Kennedy was bowled by Calthorpe. Day, number three, was this time spared the unplayable ball, and had demonstrated something of his good eye and off-side strokes, before he was caught off a big hit; and the opener Bowell had almost reached his 50 when he pulled a catch to square-leg. The bowler in each case was William Quaife, that experienced purveyor of leg-breaks. Tennyson's efforts to deal with the leg-break – aided by Calthorpe's observations – caused some amusement before the day ended. At the end Tennyson and Mead were still there, but 98 for 3 was half-way only to a score which would make Warwickshire bat again. At the end of the day a well-timed collection for Howell's benefit brought in over £24.

On the new morning, much depended on a long innings from one of them. Especially so from Mead, he of the leathery, mock-doleful countenance, the cap-tugging, foot-tapping routine at the batting crease, and the broadest bat in the business – 'The Tempered Edge Blade' which, as the advertisement proclaimed, had scored 182 against the Aussies the previous year. More venturesome, if also more vulnerable, would be Tennyson. Play started with a provocative gesture by Calthorpe, as he opposed the Hampshire captain with Quaife's leg-breaks – and with good reason, for Tennyson played the first over of his known aversion uncertainly, and to the last ball almost played on. At the other end, Howell had opened up; in his second over a fast one got through Tennyson to drop from his pad and roll against the stumps. The bails did not fall. The Hon. Calthorpe, never slow to miss the trick, came forward to make a careful examination of the stumps that had failed to offer up the Hon. Tennyson.

In half an hour 29 runs had been added when, almost out of the blue, Mead's middle stump was thrown out of the ground by the best of deliveries from Howell; it was the fast bowler's 50th wicket of a season scarcely one and a half months old. And then, on the hour, Calthorpe replaced Howell and with his second ball had Tennyson caught in the slips. The Warwickshire captain could be permitted his smile. At 152 for 5, still some 50 runs short of an innings defeat, Tennyson's 500 seemed rather distant, the £10 well wagered, a golf match in the afternoon a good idea after all.

Now Calthorpe changed ends to replace Quaife, while bringing back Howell. But the terrible pair of the previous afternoon now made little impression. It was soon to seem that Warwickshire had spent their ammunition on the necessary objective of removing Mead and his captain. Confronting them now was Brown with his soldiering build, honest, oak-dark features, and the reputation for being able to take apart fast bowlers. The left-hander, however, had not made many runs this season; and on this day his job was clearly to hold tight. So he did, as in half an hour he and Newman added what, to Edgbaston spectators, seemed a most tedious 21. But it saw off Howell and Calthorpe. The slow bowlers came back, and Newman presented a simple caught and bowled to Quaife; his successor, Shirley, stayed to lunch, when the score was 188 for 6.

Afterwards, Howell and Calthorpe once again attacked. Again, they failed to break through. Calthorpe came off soon enough for Quaife; Brown, taking a single off Howell, made sure that Warwickshire had to bat again. That milestone, perhaps, brought some belief to the Hampshire batting. Brown arrived at his 50 after two hours' batting – slow, but he was getting most of the runs being made. The 250 mark was reached, Shirley was dropped at mid-on, and then almost straightaway given lbw for 29. The partnership had added 85, and shown the way. It had also drained the thin Warwickshire attack, and enervated their fieldsmen; and although the new batsman McIntyre was soon out at 274 for 8, the ball was not beating the bat very much at all now.

Brown steadily continued to collect his runs, and he had the provoking habit of taking many singles, constantly pulling the fieldsmen out and in for left- and right-hander. Brown indeed took a lot of short singles, but never any real risks. He was not in great form, though ultimately working his way towards it. *Gathering* his runs like this, he rather deceptively took only an hour to go on from 50 to a hundred. Hampshire were also a hundred ahead. Brown's partner was Walter Livsey, who customarily batted with the painstaking diligence of his off-field employment, as valet to Lord Tennyson. Now, anxiously gnawing his glove before each delivery, but earnestly getting into line, he caused the Midland spectators to recall that the previous year against Worcestershire he had helped add 192 for the 10th wicket.

The rest of the day belonged to the two batsmen. Calth and Howell had bowled themselves out; with the 400 rolling up, and seven bowlers in all being tried, the attack began to look pitifully weak, and the fielding shoddy. Brown, beginning to indulge his favourite stroke, his wristy 'whip' to leg, continued now at a run-a-minute off his own bat, making his first substantial score of the season worth 172 before one of the occasional bowlers hit his stumps. He had come to the wicket at 127 for 4 and was out at 451 for 9. His ninth-wicket partnership with Livsey had added 177. And in the final 20 minutes the 10th wicket happily enough added another 24 runs, with the patient Livsey ending the day on 81 and Hampshire, 475 for 9, not far short of Tennyson's 500.

Warwickshire told themselves that the runs they would need, something under 300, ought still to be well within their capability. 'Slow but sure' would be the maxim. But Hampshire persisted yet further in the morning. Livsey proceeded – with a solidity which was subsequently to earn him an opening role – to his 100, his first in a career which had begun eight years previously; and the stroke which gave it to him also brought up the 500. Still Tennyson refused to declare. It was after 12 o'clock and number 11 Boyes had 29, the last-wicket stand was worth 70, and the Hampshire total was 521 when Boyes was bowled with a ball that kept low. The bowler was Howell who, following his first innings five overs for six wickets, had in the second bowled 53 overs for 156 runs and three wickets. So, Warwickshire had to make 314 to win, with not a lot of time in which to do it. The balance of confidence had now shifted. Warwickshire lost their first wicket at two, got up to 77 with the second; then lost three wickets at 85, another at 89, and in the face of a rampant fielding side were utterly done for. Tennyson kept his favourites Kennedy and Newman wheeling away, and took pleasure in surrounding the batsmen with a hardly necessary number of close-catching fieldsmen. Ultimately bowled out for 158, Warwickshire had been beaten by the comfortable margin of 155 runs, by the same side they had dismissed for 15. No wonder the Hon. Tennyson was seen performing a highland fling in the showers that evening.

Meeting again later in the season on their own soil, Hampshire made sure to reproduce only the best form of their Edgbaston match. Batting second, they scored 553, Mead making an undefeated 211, and won this match by an innings and 178.

N. H.

NES-STORMING AT MELBOURNE

Australia v England, Melbourne, December 1911

There would be many options for the batting performance superior to all others, and though someone recently devised a complicated formula – state of match, state of pitch, assessment of bowling strength, etc – there can be no universal satisfaction in the matter. It falls back always on personal choice. So it does with bowling, though the choice is narrower. And the deeds of a particular man which have been handed down from the early years of the twentieth century are still unsurpassed. Strong persuasion would be needed to unseat as the greatest bowling feat that of S. F. Barnes for England against Australia at Melbourne in the second Test match of the 1911–12 series.

England had lost the first Test, at Sydney, by 146 runs. For Australia, Victor Trumper had scored 113 – a subdued innings judged against his usual classy flamboyance – and Roy Minnett had made 90 in his first Test innings; the googly bowler, H. V. Hordern, a doctor (though of dentistry) like Minnett, took 12 for 175 in the match. It was to be England's – and MCC's – only defeat of the tour.

The touring team had been led by P. F. Warner – but only as far as the first match, at Adelaide, where he made 151 against South Australia. Then the illness which had developed on the voyage out got the better of him and he was invalided for the rest of the tour. It was only at Melbourne, on the first morning of that historic match, that he left his sick-bed to watch his men play. He was carried into the pavilion by the MCC manager, Tom Pawley, and the Australian giant Warwick Armstrong, who had already been dismissed, *after* Barnes's magic spell. Was there anything wrong with the pitch? Warner had asked. Nothing at all, Armstrong replied. It was just magnificent bowling.

Barnes was already 38 years of age. He had been 'discovered' by Archie MacLaren 10 years earlier, when Barnes was a professional with Burnley and had played only six first-class matches between 1895 and 1901, three for Warwickshire and three for Lancashire. Bowling to MacLaren in the Old Trafford nets proved to the captain beyond all doubt that here was a man who would trouble not only club and county batsmen, but international batsmen too. The cricket world was stunned when Barnes's name appeared in the side to tour Australia under MacLaren in 1901–02. A knee injury hampered him during the series, but in the three Tests in which he appeared he took 19 wickets at 17 apiece, and topped the England averages.

He toured Australia again in 1907–08, taking 24 wickets at 26.08, though his career in first-class county cricket ended as early as 1903, in which season – his second full season for the county – he took 131 wickets at 17.85 for Lancashire. From then onwards he was to play for Staffordshire, being unable to agree terms with Lancashire. There was a whisper, also, that his fellow-players at Old Trafford were unhappy at playing with a man who was unforgiving and almost vindictive in the matter of dropped catches off his bowling.

This was the man, then, tall, long-armed, with gaunt, granite-like features, who used the new ball at Melbourne after Clem Hill had won the toss for Australia and chosen to bat. In the first Test Barnes was deprived of the new ball by Warner's deputy as captain, Johnny Douglas. Barnes did not take kindly to this, and whether or not Douglas was a better bowler with a shiny ball than one that had been used took second place as an argument to whether or not he should have placed Barnes's prickly temperament foremost in his considerations.

Lesson learnt, Douglas gave the first over to the young Warwickshire left-arm fastish swing bowler Frank Foster, who bowled a maiden to Charlie Kelleway, the dour Australian opener, and then called up the dark, menacing figure of Sydney Francis Barnes.

It had been an uncomfortable few days for the Staffordshire man, who had felt 'very ill'. He had woken in the night soaked in sweat, and felt in grave doubt that he would be able to play for England. It was one of the Australians who came to his temporary assistance. When he decided that a bottle of whisky would help, Syd Gregory, the diminutive Test veteran, got it for him. On the morning of the match he could stand, but still felt well below par. 'However', he told his biographer, Leslie Duckworth, many years later, 'although I felt weak I was able to play and when I got the ball in my hands I had a curious feeling that I could do anything with it. I very nearly did.'

Barnes ran in from the railway end and bowled to Warren Bardsley, a solidly-built left-hander – one of the best ever to play for Australia. Warner described Barnes's action: 'A few steps then a couple of strides with both feet off the ground together, and the ball is delivered with concentration and marked energy.'

Bardsley played it on to the heel of his boot from where it rebounded into the stumps. Australia one down for none. The captain, Clem Hill, another very eminent left-hander, famed not only for his huge scores for South Australia and for his country but for consecutive innings of 99, 98, and 97 in the Tests against England 10 years earlier. Often he had shown he was just the man for a crisis. The pitch was firm and seemed to harbour a great many runs, but the dull morning offered an inducement to the bowlers. It usually did in Melbourne, even though the ball took on a slight greasiness when it was hit off the square. Hill settled down grimly, but was not able to make much sense out of Barnes's whipping deliveries which changed course late in their journey. Five runs accrued, two of them to the tall, upright, and inscrutable Kelleway, before that batsman missed one and the shrill, eager shout was answered by the umpire with an upraised finger. Two down for five.

Armstrong walked out, a large man, though still some way short of the 20-stone character who was to lead Australia to eight successive victories over England after the First World War. Here was a matching of the heavyweights – in spirit as well as flesh, for, like Barnes, Armstrong's uncompromising attitude and occasional outburst of acerbity persuaded many in the vicinity to keep a cautious verbal distance from him. Armstrong was often solid as a liner (he became known as 'the Big Ship'), and here was the ultimate test for his technique. His nerve had never been in question.

But it was Clem Hill's turn to face the guillotine. His head didn't roll at the first drop. His agony consisted of an off-break (to him, a left-hander), an in-swinger, an away-swinger which he let go, and, the last ball of a memorable over, one which moved a lot off the pitch (some reports said leg to off, some off to leg) and bowled him as he swung desperately at it. The crowd was generous in its applause, though Australia lay sick and sorry at 8 for three wickets; last man 4, Barnes 3 for 1.

Victor Trumper, thought by most cricketers to be the most

gifted batsman ever produced by Australia and perhaps anywhere in the world, came in at number five. Trumper – the immortal Victor – had just turned 34, and this was to be his final Test series, though no one knew it. At the end of this series Australia were to tour England, playing in a triangular tournament along with South Africa. But Trumper was not to tour with them, for he and five other leading players were to become involved in a wrangle with the Board of Control over the appointment of the manager, and the dissenting six, unable to compromise, were left out. Three years later, the Great War having already begun, Trumper died from Bright's Disease, mourned as much as any cricketer – or war hero.

The 1902 Trumper might just – *just* – have stood a chance of repelling England's brisk and teasing attack, but the 1911 model fought merely to exist. Barnes counted it something of a triumph just to keep him quiet, 'which was as good as bowling many men out'.

Armstrong, who had scored four off Foster, was Barnes's next victim. He played back to a fast leg-break ('I *spun* the ball; I never used to *cut* it!' Barnes frequently asserted in disdain, twirling his long fingers, even when nearing the end of his days, aged 94, on Boxing Day 1967). The ball clipped the outside edge of Armstrong's bat and was well caught by E. J. 'Tiger' Smith, the Warwickshire wicket-keeper, who replaced Surrey's Herbert Strudwick behind the stumps for this, the first of his 11 Tests. It is interesting to note that apart from Barnes, several others in this England team lived to ripe ages. Strudwick died in 1970 aged 90, Wilfred Rhodes in 1973 aged 95, (Sir) Jack Hobbs in 1963 aged 81, and in 1975 Frank Woolley turned 88, and wicket-keeper Smith at 89 was England's oldest Test veteran.

Smith's catch made Australia 11 for four wickets, and S. F. Barnes had taken 4 for 1. There was a 10-minute stoppage for rain just before lunch, but no further casualties, Australia lunching meekly at 32 for 4, Trumper 13, Vernon Ransford, a Victorian left-hander, 8. Barnes had been relieved when the feeling of sickness returned to overwhelm him. 'I'll have to chuck it', he told Douglas. 'I can hardly see the other end.' He rested with the astonishing figures of nine overs, six maidens, three runs, four wickets, the product of an hour and 10 minutes' labours.

Had Barnes been able to continue there is no telling where Australia's humiliation would have ended, or what incredible figures he might have achieved.

After the interval, Frank Foster chipped in with a wicket – an illustrious wicket – that of Trumper. The ball came in fast 'with the arm' from outside off stump and bowled him. Five down for 33.

Barnes then had Minnett dropped at third slip before he had scored, but claimed his wicket when he lifted one to cover and the reliable Hobbs held the catch: 38 for 6. Barnes now had 5 for 6 off 11 overs (seven maidens). No one could realistically blame the pitch – nor, for that matter, bad batting. He had utilised a slight cross breeze from leg, bowled a perfect length, and, coming down from his great height, the ball described a dangerous course all the way. Old men in the pavilion could recall no better performance.

Barnes continued to bowl superbly, but a resistance was managed at last, by Ransford and Hordern. Ransford made 43, and was eventually caught behind off Hitch, and Cotter, the fast bowler, stayed with Hordern while 17 more were added. Carter, Australia's wicket-keeper, came in, and Barnes annoyed a section of the crowd (total 26,000) by taking his time in placing the field. The booing grew in volume as he called for an extra slip fielder, and, having had enough, he threw the ball to the ground and folded his arms. Warner, the indisposed captain, watched it all from the Committee Room, and wrote afterwards: 'Barnes is a man of moods, but a good fellow. He is sensitive to a degree, and yet simple. He does not understand the Australian crowd like many others before him, and they do not understand him.'

Certainly the Australian batsmen did not understand him this day.

He took no more wickets in the innings. Australia revived to make 184 – Hordern 49 not out, Carter 29, last man Whitty 14 – and England were 38 for 1 at the end of half an hour's batting that evening, after which there was a huge smoking concert to commemorate 50 years of English-Australian international cricket. Barnes had timed his devastation cleverly.

The match was won by eight wickets, England making 219 with comparative ease and Hobbs notching the first of his record 12 centuries against Australia. 'Young Jack' Hearne, still under 21, made a lovely 114 in the first innings, and Armstrong made 90 for Australia in their second innings of 299, the highest of the match.

So the series was level at one-all, and England went on to win all the remaining three Tests. Barnes and Foster maintained their initiative with the ball, and finished with 66 of the

95 wickets that fell to English bowling during the five Tests – Barnes 34 at 22.88 and Foster 32 at 21.62.

These were startling figures, and Barnes was to better them in the two series to follow – his last, as it happened. In the six Tests of 1912 in England against both Australia and South Africa he took 39 wickets at 10.35 – though he did not bowl a single ball in the wet Old Trafford Test against Australia. In fact 34 of those wickets came at the expense of the South Africans: 11 in the first Test, 10 in the second, and 13 in the third.

The carnage went on in South Africa during the 1913–14 tour: 10 in the first Test, 17 in the second, eight in the third, 14 in the fourth. He missed the final Test. That temperament of his intruded again. But in the course of just 27 Test matches between 1901 and 1914 he piled up 189 wickets at 16.43 apiece. Had he played in the other 32 Tests during that time which he missed through injury, oversight, and unavailability he might have doubled that figure. Had there been a West Indies, a New Zealand, an India, a Pakistan to play against he might have trebled it. He implied this, in a manner to which one could take no exception, more than once in his later years. And if he had bowled always with the fire and the skill – always accompanied by the little puff of luck without which most sporting excellence is impossible – that he displayed at Melbourne on 30 December 1911, his Test career figures would for all time be beyond the reach of any other mortal.

A. T.

DAY OF DISTRESS

South Africa v New Zealand, Johannesburg,
December 1953

After the first day's play South Africa were 259 for 8, and the New Zealanders were on top of the world. The four-man seam attack of Blair, Reid, Overton, and MacGibbon had bowled their hearts out, gained persistent movement off the pitch, and had the South African batsmen on the back foot all day. The possibility that for South Africa Neil Adcock and his new partner Ironside might do even better could for the moment be pushed out of mind. For a country who had never won a Test match, who had been thrashed in the first Test of this series (437 to 230 and 149), to have the South Africans almost all out for 259 was a fine achievement. The night of Christmas Eve, and Christmas Day, were well celebrated. Boxing Day – the Saturday – was keenly anticipated.

But Christmas evening brought news of the most ghastly nature: of a disaster in the heart of New Zealand's North Island, at Tangiwai, an express train packed with Christmas travellers plunging into a flooded river with the loss of over 150 lives. By the morning, Bob Blair had received a cable telling him of the death of his fiancée at Tangiwai.

It was a sad group of cricketers who arrived at Ellis Park on Saturday morning. Blair had stayed behind at the hotel and it was announced that he had withdrawn from the Test. Flags of both countries flew at half-mast. Nevertheless, a Boxing Day crowd of 23,000, the largest of the whole season, had gathered to watch Test cricket in weather made to order, a Rand heatwave. And New Zealand's immediate job was to claim the last two South African wickets. It was soon enough done. Twelve runs were added before Ironside was bowled by Reid and Adcock was run-out.

These two bowlers now prepared for their turn with the ball, on an Ellis Park which was typically well-grassed. Perhaps the shape of the stadium bowl made it so; and the luxury of being able to grow the grass just for a few cricket matches; encouraged by the demand of the day for 'more lively wickets'. Even two days after the start of the match the matted grass still held some of its greenness. Jack Cheetham, who with reluctance chose to bat on the first day, had this morning decided against using a roller – fearing it would bring up moisture to make life difficult for his own tail-end batsmen, then ease for the New Zealand innings. In turn, the New Zealanders reacted by delaying the entrance of their most accomplished strokemaker, Bert Sutcliffe. For the first time on the tour the left-hander did not open. Instead they sent in Murray Chapple with captain Rabone.

Adcock bowled the first over. Chapple stabbed one ball down through vacant third man for four. Another lifted past the bat. Another cut back off the pitch and brought an appeal for lbw. Adcock, very tall and genuinely quick, needed to have only two types of delivery on a pitch like this: his stock-in-trade, the in-cutter, which he had a reputation of being able to activate quite venomously, balanced by the straight ball just short of a length which by contrast was effectively an away-swinger and which might also lift. His partner Ironside was less fearsome than his striking name, but a most effective seam and swing bowler. With the last ball of his first over Ironside produced a perfect lifting out-swinger and Rabone edged low into the sure hands of Endean at first slip. In Adcock's second over Chapple gained another jabbed four but then fell to the archetypal Adcock delivery, the ball whipping from the off, and lifting, to strike him on the gloves and then to fall from his body on to the stumps. New Zealand were 9 for 2 in the third over. So much for their strategy. Sutcliffe was in already.

Adcock's first ball to the left-handed Sutcliffe was on line, beat the batsman's hurried stroke and brought a demonstrative appeal for lbw. The second was much shorter, lifting, and Sutcliffe ducked it. The third, not quite so short, flew from the pitch; Sutcliffe had evidently been thinking of the hook, started to swing but abandoned it almost as quickly, turned away, and ducked his head – but too late, the ball hit him over the left ear and he spun away to the ground. A stretcher was brought out but eventually Sutcliffe left the field with the assistance of Rabone, who had dashed out, and a couple of fieldsmen.

Matt Poore, the number three batsman, was facing Adcock for the first time on the tour, and not enjoying the experience. With him John Reid – the outstanding batsman of this tour –

was making no progress at all. All he could do while being hit five times by Adcock was manage to smile. He had made three runs in 25 minutes when he got an edge to Adcock and Endean dived for another brilliant slip catch, this time seeming to snatch the ball up after a deflection from Waite's gloves. New Zealand were 23 for 3.

The experienced, commonsense Lawrie Miller came to the wicket. The first ball he faced from Adcock hit him heavily on the chest. As when Reid was being struck, there were cries, even from the partisans, of 'Take him off!' In truth, though, it did not seem that Adcock was deliberately bowling short, but that the wicket was making an outstanding fast bowler a vicious one on this day. Lawrie Miller gallantly faced Adcock again, and took a single off the next ball, but he was obviously in distress; indeed he was coughing blood. Cheetham and an umpire persuaded him to leave the field – from whence he was taken, like Sutcliffe, to hospital.

With the scoreboard showing just 28 for 3, the seventh batsman now made his way to the wicket. This left-hander, John Beck, had been just 18 years old when, without having played any first-class cricket, he was sensationally selected for this tour; and now after a first-class career of just four matches he was playing in his first Test – facing a fast bowler, on a green wicket, who had just sent two batsmen to hospital. He looked as precocious as his age: slim, pale, good-looking. But not vulnerable; he also had the confidence of youth. The ball found his bat a little more often than it found his team-mates'. Then, against Ironside, he let loose a glorious off-side drive to the fence. It was certainly the shot of the morning. It was the only shot of the morning.

At 35, Adcock got another ball to lift sharply and come back, almost cutting in half Poore who, like Chapple, saw the ball drop from his chest on to the stumps. Poore had made 15. New Zealand were 35 for 4 in an hour. Even before lunchtime, the eighth of 10 batsmen was at the wicket. Frank Mooney, the wicket-keeper, stayed with Beck for the 10 minutes to the interval, when the score was 41 for 4.

During lunch, the press were told that neither Sutcliffe nor Miller was likely to go in again. After lunch, Beck square drove Adcock for four. The fast bowler was rested after three overs, indicating that the pitch might have lost some of its venom. Ironside and Murray, though, were both swinging and seaming the ball disconcertingly. Murray kept forcing Beck away from his favourite front foot, and finally got the edge he was working for. Beck had played a remarkably competent innings, yet it was a measure of the scale of New Zealand's difficulty that his innings was in fact a matter of less than an hour for 16 runs; and their position was really not much improved, at 59 for 5.

The ninth New Zealand batsman, MacGibbon, was now awaited. Through the pavilion gate, however, came Lawrie Miller, to sustained applause. It was against medical advice that he was continuing his innings, and it was apparent, as he played, that he was still in some discomfort. But he got solidly behind the ball; and twice he pulled Murray high out to square-leg for four. With Mooney continuing dour and reasonably safe, New Zealand were once again beginning to make fractional progress. A cover drive for two by Mooney took him to the highest score of the innings – 17. Miller's brave contribution was of the same order – 14 runs – when at 82 Ironside cut one sharply back into him and hit leg stump. Six wickets down for 82, and the follow-on target of 121 seemed daunting. Each struggling effort at recovery was being suffocated with cruel regularity.

MacGibbon was again awaited. Instead, Sutcliffe's blond head appeared, cotton wool and padding strapped over his left ear. His face was grey. He was batting again after collapsing twice – once on the pitch and once again at the hospital. If the applause for Miller's return had been whole-hearted, for Sutcliffe's battered figure it was overwhelming.

Yet to open his score, he faced Ironside. He opened it third ball, picking up one on leg stump and whipping it over square-leg for six. Next over, he lifted Ironside to long-on for three, then hooked again for four. The crowd rejoiced to see it, but for the fielding captain, Cheetham, admiration was tempered with discretion. He placed two men on the leg-side fence. On 17, against Murray, Sutcliffe again went for a big hit and skied the ball a towering height over deep point. Tayfield, twisting and turning and following the flight back, dropped the chance. There was some cheering from the crowd at this, and it did not all come from the small non-European section.

The action had caused Sutcliffe's head-dressing to slip. An ambulance man, summoned to the middle, put a full bandage around his head. Then Sutcliffe faced up as his antagonist, Adcock, returned to bowl to him. He took a single, Mooney took a single, and then Sutcliffe square-cut crackingly for four. Even if he would never play Adcock with confidence again (or any other bowler as quick) it was obvious that right now he was going to, with a cold fury. So at the other end Cheetham brought on Tayfield. A slow bowler – perhaps the most successful off-spinner in contemporary cricket – was the most likely to trap the hitter.

Tayfield's first ball to Sutcliffe was an inviting length. With an unhurried stroke it was lifted high and perfectly straight for six. That the follow-on had been saved with this stroke seemed incidental to the continuing excitement; and two balls later, Sutcliffe again swung long and easily for six over long-off. The fieldsmen on the fence were irrelevant. Tayfield now pitched shorter and Sutcliffe, as if he knew it before the ball was bowled, idly dispatched it for four through square-leg.

In 39 minutes Sutcliffe and Mooney had added 50, Sutcliffe contributing the runs and Mooney the time. The 'keeper played Adcock obdurately – as frustrating for the bowler as it was painful for himself, as he three times turned his back on a ball and was hit, once by a full toss, once on the hand, once on the rump, and three times the bat dropped from his hand. Having batted throughout the afternoon session, taking his score up to 35 in an innings of priceless defiance, he accompanied Sutcliffe into tea with New Zealand's total 138 for 6.

In the second over after tea Mooney's innings was over with no addition to the score, as Ironside completely beat and bowled him. MacGibbon, after a long wait, now came and went – to another sharp slip catch by Endean, off Ironside. Guy Overton came in – virtually last man – and played down the line, while Sutcliffe started a final thrash. A fourth six was struck against Tayfield, and an intended fifth was almost caught, but dropped, by Murray at long-off. Overton had played but a handful of deliveries, and had not scored, when he was caught off Ironside. The scoreboard showed 154, and the players began to leave the field. They stopped at the sight of the crowd stirring around the pavilion gate, and Bob Blair emerging on to the field. All spectators now stood up. A few applauding, emphasised the silence. As Blair walked towards the wicket, fumbling to get his batting gloves on, the other New Zealanders up in the pavilion were weeping openly; clearly distressed also were the South African fieldsmen and Sutcliffe, who walked to meet his number 11 and put an arm on his shoulder. Blair had intended not to play, but the fall of wickets in the late morning had caused him to make his own way to the ground at lunchtime; since tea he had decided to bat, because New Zealand so badly needed the runs – and someone to stay with Sutcliffe.

The partnership was brief but more vivid still than anything else on this day. Tayfield bowled again to Sutcliffe, with men on the boundary at square-leg, mid-wicket, wide long-on, long-off, and extra cover. They were again rendered helpless as Sutcliffe lifted the first ball over the fence at long-on, likewise the second, played the third, and then once more struck the ball into a frenzied crowd. A most remarkable sight: spectators at a Test match, whose team is in the field, on their feet and shouting themselves hoarse as sixes from an opposition batsman rained among them. The over was not finished yet. Sutcliffe took a single to retain the strike, and Blair faced. As for Sutcliffe, there was the strange sight of fieldsmen on the line to a batsman in distress. Blair then finished off by letting one go himself: not straight like Sutcliffe's but swung to mid-wicket, landing far into the crowd. For all the 20,000, it was the final delirium.

Twenty-five runs off Tayfield's over, a partnership of 33 in 10 minutes, and then Blair was stumped. New Zealand all out 187, Sutcliffe 80 not out. Of the 105 scored by the last four New Zealand batsmen, he had made 80, in 97 minutes; of the 53 runs that Tayfield had conceded in eight overs, he had taken 45 – in 11 strokes. It was to be reckoned one of the most spectacular innings ever played in South Africa. As he came off, head bandaged, players and crowd prepared a hero's welcome. Instead, Sutcliffe stood aside at the gate, so that Blair passed through first; and then they went clasped together into the darkness of the tunnel.

N. H.

WELL, I DECLARE

West Indies v England, Bridgetown, January 1935

The Test match played in January 1935 at Kensington Oval, Bridgetown, Barbados between West Indies and England is rivalled by only one other in the drama of the timing of the captains' declarations, and that was at Brisbane in 1950, when Australia made 228 and 32 for 7 declared to beat England 68 for 7 declared and 122. Rain, in both instances, was the cause of the chaos.

The England side in West Indies in 1934–35 was led by R. E. S. Wyatt, and though it could not have been considered the best that England could field, it contained some appreciable cricketers, such as Hammond, Hendren, Leyland, Ames, and Farnes. They played two matches before the opening Test, both against Barbados, and having survived the first, with young leg-spinner Eric Hollies taking eight wickets, the touring side gathered its strength during the second, with Wally Hammond striking 281 not out and adding 122 for the last wicket with 'Big Jim' Smith (83) in a frantic three-quarters of an hour. The match was eventually spoilt by heavy incessant rain during Barbados' follow-on innnings. Three days later the Test match began, but it had rained again on the previous night, and, when Wyatt won the toss from G. C. 'Jack' Grant, he asked West Indies to bat. It was plain to everyone that batting would be a precarious business.

Learie Constantine, still not returned from a coaching engagement in India, was missing from the home team, but the great Jamaican batsman George Headley was in, together with fast bowlers Leslie Hylton and 'Manny' Martindale, whose journey by ship had taken nigh on a fortnight. Grant's brother, Rolph, was in, as were Clifford Roach, who in old age was destined to lose both legs. Ellis 'Puss' Achong, the only Chinaman to play Test cricket, was chosen for his slow bowling; Christiani, who came from the mainland of British Guiana with Jones, was West Indies' wicket-keeper; and Carew and the 22-year-old Sealey were Barbados' own representatives.

The tall, dark-haired Essex fast bowler Ken Farnes began the attack after a shower had delayed the start for 20 minutes after the pitch had been rolled. It was soon apparent that the bounce of the ball was not to be trusted in the least. Some deliveries shot through low while the majority kicked, making the short-leg positions and gully premium catching areas. The art of taking the bat away from the ball was more often than not of greater importance than putting bat to ball. After only one run had been posted, Carew was caught by Errol Holmes at long-leg off a solid stroke before he had scored, and at 11 Roach was caught by George Paine at short-leg also off Farnes. Jones was caught at short cover by Leyland, and Paine snapped up a second catch when Sealey lifted a ball from Farnes to short-leg. Jim Smith was unlucky in obtaining no results from the other end, and after an hour Hollies came on. In his second over he had the West Indies captain caught by Patsy Hendren at slip. The score swayed drunkenly at 31 for 5, and the chief destroyer, Farnes, had 4 for 15.

The lunch interval brought with it much animated discussion about the sensations of the morning, the locals taking refuge and consolation only in the fact that George Headley, in the consideration of many of them the finest batsman in the whole world, was still unbeaten, with 13 by his name, having come in at the fall of the first wicket.

Rolph Grant stayed with Headley until 49, when he became Hollies' second victim, caught by Hammond. But it was now apparent that the pitch was drier, and while still far removed from a batsman's paradise, it offered much less assistance to the faster bowlers. Leslie Hylton, the big Jamaican fast bowler, who was to be hanged in 1955 for the murder of his wife, now pushed the score along with Headley, stealing swift singles, launching into some powerful hits, and all the while chewing a toothpick. The total was built up to 81 before he went out to Paine, missed, and was stumped by Ames for 15, which was to be the second highest score after Headley's 44.

Headley survived two hours all told, being missed twice but showing over after over that he was in a class all of his own. His downfall was tragic in its unnecessary nature. He thought he saw a quick single, Christiani refused, and Headley slipped on the greasy turf as he turned to get back.

Achong was stumped off Paine without scoring, and last

man Martindale managed nine runs before becoming Paine's third wicket, caught by Leyland running round the boundary of this small ground. West Indies were all out for 102, and now it was England's turn to face the music, though the melody had the gaiety of a calypso only to bowlers and fielders.

England finished that first day at 81 for 5. Much of the spitefulness had receded; in fact, the pitch was then as sedate as it was ever going to be throughout the match. Yet the West Indians, spearheaded by Martindale and Hylton, bowled with fire and determination. The captain, Bob Wyatt, was scooped up at short-leg by Rolph Grant off Martindale for eight, and the same bowler took left-hander Leyland's valuable wicket for three. Worse followed: Hendren (3) parried another fast one from Martindale and was snapped up by Rolph Grant, standing very close at short-leg: 28 for 3. The same fielder chipped in with a wicket next, having Ames lbw for eight, and Wyatt altered the batting order by sending in Jim Smith in the hope he would hit England out of trouble. He was caught by Jones deep on the leg side off Hylton for a duck.

At last Hammond found someone to stay with him. Jack Iddon of Lancashire, who was to die 11 years later in a car accident, held an end for the remaining half hour, finishing 14 not out, with Hammond a praiseworthy 43, the hardest innings, by his own estimation, that he ever played in his long and highly distinguished career.

What should happen after the curtain descended on the first act but further torrential rain! Next day the pitch was saturated, and for several hours the players could only wander restlessly around the dressing-rooms while the crowd tried, sometimes unsuccessfully, to control its impatience. The captains inspected the square, treading gingerly, their shoes squelching, and at last, just before the tea interval, the pitch was declared 'fit'. Anticipation rose as all eyes switched to the centre.

Hylton bounded in and got the second ball to leap viciously at Hammond's face. The batsman stabbed at it protectively and Rolph Grant was there at short-leg to take his third catch of the innings. Errol Holmes, the Surrey captain, was out first ball, caught by Achong. Hylton had two wickets in the first three balls of the day and was on a hat trick. But he was to be denied – for the moment, at least. Wyatt, knowing full well that the pitch was virtually unplayable, decided he would rather have West Indies batting on it. Thus he declared 21 runs behind on the first innings.

Jack Grant held back his key batsmen, hoping that two or three night-watchmen would see West Indies through that evening and that the pitch would quieten next day. But Jim Smith, the big man from Middlesex, ripped out the captain's brother and Martindale, and then Achong all without a run from the bat. Hylton was then caught at gully but given 'not out', and he and Christiani saw West Indies to 33 for 3 at the close of play, called slightly early when dark clouds blotted out the sun and a second light appeal was successful. Before this spectators, changing their line of argument, had run on to the field demanding that play be suspended, even though Wyatt, in the interests of a continuation, had put his slower bowlers on. Hylton was 17 not out, and West Indies' lead was 54. More rain thundered down from the heavy skies, and soon the pitch was under water again.

The third morning brought with it a strong breeze and bright sunshine, but hours of drying were needed before play could be considered. It was after three o'clock before the match was resumed, with the same sense of nail-biting expectation.

The pressure now was distinctly upon West Indies. Inadequate batting would mean a low target for England; survival on the treacherous pitch would only allow it to quieten for the relative delectation of England in due course. Jack Grant had one of the trickiest dilemmas to deal with that any captain has known. When three wickets fell rapidly he felt it was time to manipulate the match. He declared at tea at 51 for 6, setting England 73 for victory on a 'pig' of a wicket. In all fairness, Grant's strategy could not be condemned.

Smith and Farnes had opened the bowling for England, and Smith soon bowled Christiani for 11 and had Hylton leg-before for a courageous 19. Roach and Headley saw the 50 up, but the latter, the 'Black Bradman', was caught off his thumb by Paine off Farnes without scoring, and Grant saw this as the signal to throw the gauntlet at England's feet.

Wyatt sent in the pair of huge fast bowlers who had opened his attack, saying they were the tallest men in the XI and would therefore have their facial features furthest from danger. He refrained from having the pitch rolled, fearing that any extra moisture brought up would prolong the stickiness.

Martindale, of medium height but considerable strength, opened from the pavilion end, from which most of the damage had been done throughout the contest, and Smith swung and swished at everything without getting a touch, the ball swinging away. Hylton bowled fast from the other end to Farnes, but was too short in length, wasting precious minutes. Martindale took up the attack, and this time Smith managed to get a touch – but to wicket-keeper Christiani. Having taken 5 for 15, he had now 'bagged a pair'. Holmes came in, with every other England batsman already padded up in readiness!

At eight, Farnes went, caught off a Hylton full toss by Jack Grant, and this brought in Patsy Hendren, 46 years of age and an idol in the Caribbean five years previously, when he had made a mountain of runs and won the affection of spectators with his skill and, more obviously, his happy manner. (Numerous four-year-olds named after him now inhabited the islands!) He was soon smiting Hylton for a leg-side six, but Martindale, bowling at great speed, got Holmes (6) caught at short-leg, where the wickets were falling with a kind of monotony.

Leyland made two and was taken in the same area off Martindale. This brought in England's premier batsman, Hammond, who could be held back no longer, lest he be stranded high and dry. It was 29 for 4 – 44 still needed.

Hendren and Hammond added 14 – almost a large partnership in the tense context! The rotund Middlesex man played the technically finest innings of the match, standing outside leg stump to allow many of the more disconcerting kickers to pass harmlessly by, and reacting with sharp reflexes remarkable in a man approaching his half-century of years. With the total 43, and with his score 20, Hendren couldn't cope with a yorker from Martindale, and now Paine came to do his duty. Five runs later he was out, giving Rolph Grant his fifth catch of the match, and Martindale his fifth wicket of the innings. Could the tough Jamaican bring off an heroic victory? Bob Wyatt, England's obdurate skipper, came out to defy him.

Hylton was tiring, and was getting less bounce out of the wicket, yet Grant could hardly bring in a new bowler for fear he would take time finding a length. It would also have given the batsmen a little longer to react.

Hammond was now batting with the resource of a genius. Sometimes he withdrew his blade when it seemed he had to get a touch to the flying ball. Wicket-keeper and short-legs bent forward eagerly, but were denied. Sometimes the Gloucestershire man would stand up to his full height and hammer the rising ball with a horizontal bat through mid-off. England were approaching the magic figure. They were winning the match.

And so it was. Martindale and Hylton bowled their hearts out to the bitter end, through 16.3 overs between them, Martindale taking 5 for 22, Hylton, unable to repeat his first-innings dominance, 1 for 48.

Hammond finished it in the grand manner, stepping boldly out to Martindale and smashing the ball well over long-off for six. England were home by four wickets in a match whose scores had defied interpretation by many cricket followers in other parts of the world who were unaware of the truly evil qualities of a rain-affected West Indian pitch. Those who had taken part and those who had watched in the flesh were never to forget.

Jack Grant, the unlucky home captain, was not to be allowed to forget the result. He was blamed, even villified in the streets, and it would have been slight comfort to him to know that his opposing leader would have acted identically in the heat of the battle. Wyatt was to write some years afterwards: 'It would have been nearer to the truth if he'd been described as the man who nearly won the Test match. In my view his decision was absolutely right. There were signs of the weather clearing up that night and if it had done there was every reason to suppose that the wicket would have been a perfectly good one the next morning.'

Wyatt himself had colourful memories of the end of the match. As Hammond's six sailed into the crowd, a group of spectators ran out and lifted Wyatt on to their shoulders. Unfortunately they held his legs but let his head trail only inches from the ground. 'All I could see', he recalled, 'on that extraordinary trip to the pavilion, surrounded by cheering, shouting, and enthusiastic West Indians, was their feet.'

By the fourth Test, Wyatt had added memories of the tour that were anything but welcome. Having put West Indies in again on Trinidad's jute matting wicket, he lost the second Test when Constantine took the final wicket, Leyland, with the penultimate ball of the match. The third Test, at Georgetown, was drawn, but during the fourth – the decider – at Kingston, Jamaica, Wyatt was struck horribly on the jaw by a ball from Martindale. The result was a compound fracture, and the result of the match was an innings victory for West Indies (Headley 270 not out), who registered their first-ever series victory.

The Barbados 'declaration match', however, was the battle that was to live on as a 'museum piece'. As a test of nerve, as a study in tactics, it remains unique, and will forever be kept in spirit in a bottle in cricket's memory vaults.

A. T.

LAKER'S TEST

England v Australia, Manchester, July 1956

The wicket always attracts keen interest on the day before a Test match starts: none more so than this one, with Australia having made few runs in the series and been twice bowled out cheaply at Leeds to lose the third Test by an innings. This time there was not much grass to be seen on the pitch. One interested observer, Sir Donald Bradman, had high hopes for it. It was just what the Australians had been waiting for, he remarked; they only needed to win the toss and they would make a packet of runs. Jim Laker, to whom he made the comment, felt very differently. Laker had been deceived by the Leeds pitch, which wore quickly, but he was sure from one look at this Old Trafford strip that it would take turn early in the match. There was too little grass to bind it solidly.

As it happened, Australia did not win the toss. If they had, how many might they have made on a wicket taking turn on the first day? Judging by subsequent events, perhaps 250. At any rate, England batted with profit on a wicket which was slow from the outset and gave no assistance at all to their best bowlers, Lindwall and Miller. On the opening day the spinners Johnson and Benaud did a great deal of bowling, and almost all the bowling on the second morning, as England raced to 459 all out. Already, even on the first day, some balls were seen to cause dust puffs as they pitched. It was subsequently pointed out that these, which were leg-spinners from Benaud, had pitched in other bowlers' follow-through marks. Even so, one would not expect such fringe marks to cause dust on the first day of a Test – not if the wicket was hard and well-bound. Laker and Lock must have had twitching fingers by the time they took the ball on Friday afternoon, after Statham and Bailey had bowled but 10 overs between them.

The durable Australian openers, McDonald and Burke, remained calm while the spinners operated for half an hour and then changed ends. Laker was now at the Stretford End which was to remain almost entirely his until the end of the match – a match perhaps determined in his 10th over when he had Australia's most reliable batsman, McDonald, caught in the leg trap, and then immediately bowled Neil Harvey. The ball which got McDonald unsettled the batsman in its flight; the one which got the left-handed Harvey was an uncompromising 'biter' pitching on leg stump and racing past an uncertain bat to hit the top of the off. Though Burke and Craig played through to tea, there was no doubt that Harvey's dismissal – with the batsman staring at the pitch in disbelief – had shaken the Australians. Further discussion during the interval surely served to illuminate, in the Australian mind, the spectre of Jim Laker.

Before this day, of course, he had shown himself a quite ruthless destroyer. In 1950 he had made a nonsense of the Test trial at Bradford by taking eight wickets for two runs in 14 overs. Earlier this season, he had already taken all 10 wickets in an innings against the Australians – and on a wicket which was by no means nasty. That was done at The Oval, playing for his county Surrey. There was something about Jim Laker's manner at the bowling crease which bespoke both Surrey and his native Yorkshire: the solid, capable, slightly stiff, slightly self-aware walk of the Metropolitan constable, and the taciturnity of the northcountryman. Though he came up to the wicket with the short, trotting steps of the slow spinner, the delivery was emphatic. His front foot stamped down, his lips tightened, his right arm came straight down with military vigour, as if ordering arms. And the head stayed high and still.

It was more than just a classic *picture*. His perfect side-on position – pivoted on his right foot, looking over his left shoulder at the batsman, left arm stock-straight above his head with the hand bent flat, pointing the way – provided him with the impetus and the method, if he wished to employ it, of the medium-pace swing bowler. (Indeed, there was little to separate Laker and Bedser in profile prior to delivery.) And employ it he did, especially when bowling around the wicket, to make the ball curve and float across the right-handed batsman. For that speciality, he took the hand under the ball, effecting a kind of under-spin. For another speciality he brought the hand over the ball, as if turning a valve; this ball tended to arch higher, deceiving the batsman as to its length, and then on pitching hurrying through with the top-spin. There was also an effective quicker ball, bowled with the same action. All this, of course, apart from the orthodox 'tweaked' off-break which on a receptive surface could almost, as the professionals say, turn square. It is doubtful if any off-spinner has spun the ball as much *with* as much control. At any rate, Laker's stature was now to be determined less by cricketing opinion than by unarguable statistics.

Before tea, at which point Australia were 62 for 2, Laker had bowled 13 overs. After tea, and after Lock had got Burke caught with his opening ball, Laker delivered less than four overs more to have Australia all out for 84. It was the most devastating spell of bowling in all Test cricket: seven wickets in 22 balls. It is easily said, less easy to comprehend fully – *a wicket every three balls.* He took two wickets in his 14th over, two in his 15th, one in the 16th and two again in the four balls of the 17th. Starting with the fall of McDonald, he took nine wickets for 16 runs, to finish with 9 for 37.

Like Lock, his first ball after tea won him a wicket, when young Ian Craig, who had been playing soundly to the interval, was on the back foot and clearly lbw to the off-spinner that hurried through. Following Harvey's dismissal before tea, and both not-out batsmen dismissed with their first ball afterwards, the Australians now capitulated to Laker. Mackay, mesmerised, lamely hung out his bat and gave – as if giving practice – a catch to gully. Miller, after clouting a desperate six off Lock, lunged forward and was simply taken in the leg trap. Benaud hit out, into Statham's hands at long-on, and Archer feverishly tore down the pitch to miss and be stumped. Maddocks and Johnson were both utterly deceived into hesitating on the back foot, and were bowled. Australia were all out at 10 minutes past five. They were not then to know it, but if they had only batted half as weakly, doubling the short time of their stay after tea, they would (with help from the weather) have saved this Test, and the series.

Australia had to bat again, for 65 minutes to stumps. The mood of the cricket in this period was near to anti-climax as Australia, with Burke quick-footed against the spinners, made a healthy 53 runs for one wicket. The wicket was that of Harvey, who came in when McDonald retired with knee trouble; his first ball was a full toss from Laker and he hit it straight to Cowdrey, 20 yards away at short mid-wicket. Harvey tossed his bat in the air, an eloquent gesture. He had made the first 'pair' in his life, collecting both ducks in not much more than an hour, and lasted but four balls in all.

After the end of play a number of Englishmen and Australians went out to have a look at the wicket. Those who looked and said nothing were players not engaged in this match, the Australian managers, England selectors, Lancashire's chairman and secretary. The 'pitch' found its way into most of the newspaper headlines the next morning – as it did again on Monday morning, after a damp Saturday and another two days for opinions to calm or foment. One of the most critical came back from Australia, from R. S. Whitington in the *Sunday Telegraph*: 'England's reputation for sportsmanship is right on the edge of whatever instrument was used to shear this travesty of a pitch. England should not be allowed to get away with this sort of thing any longer.' In answer to this 'petty squabble and dispute' one of the most trenchant of English defences was Denys Rowbotham's in the *Manchester Guardian*: 'The Old Trafford pitch did not assist pace and during the second day did allow Benaud, Johnson, Lock, and Laker to turn the ball. The Australian strength in attack is still pace, for Benaud and Johnson cannot use any type of English turning wicket as well as can England, which is another way of saying that they are not technically such comprehensive players. Is the logical deduction, therefore, that English groundsmen must prepare wickets which will suit the Australian hostility in attack and not expose the limitations of their batting? In this Welfare State age of all things on a platter and made easy, is a turning wicket a dishonour and no longer a challenge to personal skill?'

Other writers, however, seemed to acknowledge that strength in exploiting, or weakness in combating, the conditions did not necessarily exonerate bad conditions. *The Times* and the *Daily Telegraph* equally suggested that both sides were entitled to expect good sound batting conditions in their first innings. 'Only twice in England, and never abroad', wrote E. W. Swanton in the *Daily Telegraph*, 'can I recall Tests in which the surface of the wicket so disintegrated on the second day.' These criticisms, however, were balanced by the observation that McDonald and Burke had twice batted with reasonable success (Australia's only real failures occurring in the 55-minute capitulation spanning the Friday tea interval), that Lock had failed to take more than one wicket in 25 overs to date, and that Australia's spinners had been unable to exploit the same conditions when England's tail-enders were batting. Conclusion: Australia had suffered disappointing conditions, but they had not adapted to them very well, and Laker had exploited them magnificently.

Only three-quarters of an hour's play had been possible on the wet Saturday, Burke being picked up in Laker's leg trap for 33, and McDonald coming back in to make four of the six runs added with one shot, a square-cut off Laker. On the Monday action was again minimal as McDonald and Craig continued carefully on a damp pitch, unhelpful to bowler or batsman; in 40 minutes they added 18 before rain, and in a later period of 10 minutes another seven runs, to finish the day at 84 for 2, McDonald on 25 and Craig on 24. Only Lock had got an occasional ball to pop, and in the first period of play Laker had actually been relieved by Statham – though the off-spinner still had the only wickets to fall in this innings.

Rain continued in Manchester until five o'clock on Tuesday morning. With the wind still brisk, though, play was only 10 minutes late in starting. The pitch was sluggish: Australia needed it to stay so, England needed sunshine to give it life. McDonald and Craig played themselves in against Bailey and Laker, who subsequently made way for Lock and Oakman. Runs were of no object to Australia, who were still nearly 300 behind, but were some use to boost morale, to push one or two fielders back into deeper catching positions, and perhaps also to get a batsman to the opposite end. The real test was concentration and judgment of length. Craig, 21 years old, demonstrated near-immaculate judgment, allowing him impressive time to play his stroke.

McDonald's forte was concentration as he continued an innings, on Tuesday morning, which he started on Friday evening. To score, he mainly waited for the chance to cut; otherwise it was all forward and back defence. If, perhaps, his method was still a little too 'open' according to the English textbook, nevertheless his back play especially was more side-on than was some of his colleagues'. No doubt he was continuing to build on experience gained on his 'learning' tour to England in 1953. In the innings against Surrey where Lock took all 10 wickets, he had made 89 of Australia's 259. Now, even when the ball started to jump, he played without fault to go into lunch having, with Craig, added just 28 runs. Australia were 112 for 2. Each of them had now been batting for over four hours. Ahead stretched another four.

The clouds were clearing now, the sun shining brightly. Fifteen minutes into the afternoon session, with both batsmen having been discomforted, Laker deceived Craig in the air and then beat him off the pitch. The ball, deceptively well flighted, hurried through on pitching and struck the pads, Craig having lingered too long on the back foot. He was thus lbw, almost identically so, in each innings. Craig out for 33 – in 259 minutes – made Australia 114 for 2.

Now the brittle middle order was again revealed. Surrounded by six fieldsmen all within five yards, Mackay floundered for 10 minutes, sometimes pushing both pads at the ball like a hockey goalkeeper, before pushing the bat out to the ball leaving him and giving a catch into the middle of the slips. Like Harvey, Mackay had collected a 'pair'. Keith Miller also tried to play everything with his pads – in him an even more incongruous sight. His unwillingness to use the bat soon undid him, as he brought it into play too late on a leg-stump yorker, and was bowled. Archer went simply: playing half-back to the off-break and steering it, in effect, into the leg trap. Mackay, Miller, and Archer had all made ducks, and Australia were 130 for 6.

Meanwhile McDonald could only watch from the other end. During these overs he found himself engaged against Lock, against whom he gained occasional compensation by swinging away a short ball. Lock, in his frustration, was perhaps bowling a little too quickly; the ball was certainly leaping away off the pitch but, especially when it was bowled on the short side of a good length, it was beating the bat by too much. But judgments had to be subjective, for when Laker was bowling to McDonald the ball seemed to be turning less dangerously. The opening batsman was now well partnered by Benaud, whose method was calm – eschewing the desperate hitting of his own first innings and also the other extreme of Mackay's and Miller's pad-play. In the main, he played back; at least, he took up an early position on the back foot, determined to watch the ball for as long as possible before committing himself – only playing forward if he had to, and when he could smother the spin. It was a rational approach, if dangerous. Several batsmen had already fallen this way, bowled or lbw to the ball which was a fuller length than realised, and also imparted with top-spin. But Benaud, though driven almost on to his stumps, sometimes getting a last-minute edge on to the ball, managed to survive; he also contributed to the passing time by checking his guard at least once an over and meticulously patting down every semblance of a divot left by the previous ball. So McDonald and Benaud lasted together for an hour and 20 minutes to tea – adding 50 – during which time they caused an anxious Peter

May to switch his spinners around and to introduce Bailey and Oakman.

When the final session began Australia still had two hours to occupy with their last four wickets. No doubt the tea was an important refreshment for England's bowlers as well as a break in the Australians' concentration. With his second ball after tea Laker got McDonald to play half-cock at one that turned sharply, the ball flew from the edge and Oakman in the leg trap held his fifth catch of the game. McDonald had made 89, the same score as when he stood alone at The Oval. This time he had batted for five and a half hours, during which he had come to the wicket and taken guard for seven different passages of play, and he had not given a chance until he was out. If he had made just 11 runs more for his 100, and the match had ended a little differently, it might well have been regarded as the greatest defensive innings in Test cricket.

But McDonald had fallen, and the next two balls turned sharply, putting the Australian situation in grim perspective. For the first time in the game the pitch was taking *quick* turn. Shortly Benaud went back to Laker for the final time, to a generously flighted off-break of fullish length, and the ball nipped off through his belated stroke to bowl him. The score was 198 for 8; but now the total, and Australia's imminent defeat, had been overtaken by an incredible prospect. Laker had taken all eight wickets to fall; with nine in the first innings, his 17 in the match already equalled all first-class records. Could he gain one more? Or even the *two*? But Laker had now bowled nearly 50 overs in the innings, his spinning fingers were tired, and he was conscious of mental as well as physical strain. And there was to be no collusion with Lock, who was furiously seeking the wickets that, on this tailor-made pitch, were oddly eluding him. At any rate, England as a team were desperately hunting for the remaining two wickets, as Lindwall and Maddocks hung on. At a quarter past five they were still there, making the quarter-hour of the partnership seem a very long time. Snicks from Lindwall's bat had actually been going through the leg trap fieldsmen.

Then Lindwall stretched once more and Lock, placed the finest in the leg trap, delightedly hugged the catch. Laker had a world record. Now, after an over from Lock, he bowled to Maddocks. It was to the second ball of his 52nd over, well flighted and well up, that Maddocks – like others before him – was on the back foot when the ball hurried through on to his pads. The shout was answered by the umpire's finger and the words 'That's out'. Maddocks promptly walked to Laker and shook his hand, as the crowd flooded on to the field.

The excitement was not the demonstrative type: while spectators cheered and clapped, Laker, with as much evident emotion as any Surrey or Yorkshire man after an average working day, jog-trotted and walked briskly off the field. He had a half glass of champagne, while all the Australians crowded into the English dressing-room. Australia, all out for 203, had lost by an innings and 171, and the Ashes remained with England.

Laker's bowling had broken all sorts of records. Most of them could be disregarded, compared with his over-riding achievement in taking 19 wickets – *two* more than anyone else in a first-class cricket match, let alone a Test against Australia. Following his first innings 9 for 37 from 16.4 overs, the second innings produced 10 for 53 from 51.2 overs. The number of overs was far too high, the return of other bowlers too small from such long effort, for Laker's figures to be regarded as good fortune. Moreover, calm recollection would reveal that he gained as many wickets by deceiving batsmen in flight as he did with sharp spin into the leg trap. Still, the *figures* really were the thing. By the end, this personal epic had put arguments into perspective – or out of perspective. As sensational a topic as the pitch had been early in the Test match, his 10 second innings wickets, his 19 in the match, had transcended all arbitration.

N. H,

THE 'IMPOSSIBLE' VICTORY

Australia v England, Sydney, December 1894

A few – a very few – Australians are aware that Sir Robert Menzies, probably their country's greatest statesman, was born on 20 December 1894; and fewer still possess the somewhat useless knowledge that on that exact day there concluded in Sydney one of the most amazing Test matches of all time.

It was the first in a five-match series between Australia and England, who had been taken there by Middlesex batsman A. E. Stoddart under the auspices of the Melbourne and Sydney cricket authorities.

Andrew Stoddart had raised a strong side, the thirteenth to tour Australia, almost the best England could have fielded even at home. The Australians had a team, too, of which their followers could be proud, and by the fifth and deciding Test the nation was agog with excitement. Thousands were heading for the matches by train, steamer, on horseback, and even tramping long distances on foot. This was the series when Test cricket came of age, when the press took a new and larger interest in the game. Indeed, the *Pall Mall Gazette* spent vast sums on cabling the story daily, and it was rumoured that even Queen Victoria wanted regular reports on the progress of the English cricketers in her distant colony.

There was an abundance of fascinating cricket during the five Tests, yet the key to it was probably the unpredictable opening Test, begun with a flip of the coin by Jack Blackham, Australia's captain and wicket-keeper with spade beard. Stoddart, with kindly eyes and sweeping moustache, said as the coin spun through the warm, clear air, 'Someone will be swearing directly, Jack. I hope it's you!' He was referring to the smooth, dry pitch, which seemed to harbour a great many runs. Blackham won the toss and took first innings for the Australians, who had been practising for four days.

Tom Richardson, England's big, honest, black-haired fast bowler, soon had Australia in desperate trouble, bowling Lyons off his knee, smashing the top off Harry Trott's off stump, and yorking left-hander Joe Darling first ball in his first Test innings. Australia were 21 for three wickets, and it was up to George Giffen and Frank Iredale to perform a rescue.

This they did, adding 171 for the fourth wicket before Stoddart caught Iredale for 81. This must have brought inexpressible relief to England's wicket-keeper, Leslie Gay (who kept goal for England the previous winter). He had fumbled a return from a fieldsman when Giffen and Iredale were both at the bowler's end, dropped Giffen when he was 75, and repeated the tragedy a few minutes later; then he grassed an edge off the toiling Richardson's bowling. His confidence was in ribbons. It was as if he had let in six goals against Scotland.

Stoddart was trying all his bowlers, though Richardson and Yorkshire slow left-armer Bobby Peel bore the brunt. Peel was hit for 14 off a six-ball over by tiny Syd Gregory, Iredale's replacement, and in half an hour 53 runs were added, the ball speeding across the Sydney ground like a crazy cat's-cradle. Giffen, South Australia's answer to W. G. Grace and now going on 36, was well past his hundred, and as Gregory passed 50 and was dropped at slip, Giffen rode high on 150. The frantic half hour at the start of the day was a mere memory.

It seemed these two, having added 139, would be unseparated that evening; what records could they not smash in the morning after a good night's sleep? But Billy Brockwell, the Surrey all-rounder, chipped in by having Giffen caught by Francis Ford at slip for 161, the finest innings of his life. Australia 331 for 5, with Reedman seeing the day out with Gregory.

Stoddart had worries that evening, with Bill Lockwood's shoulder ricked, Peel and Johnny Briggs, the left-arm slow bowlers, wicketless and expensive, and Richardson unable to utilise the high bounce of the pitch. But Saturday was a bright new day, and with the grass sparkling in the sunlight, Stoddart led out his cricketers.

Richardson, refreshed, began bumping the ball all over the place. Something was bound to happen. Reedman slashed and was dropped by Brockwell; then he was struck on the head; then he retaliated by hitting Peel into the crowd, which was a ground record. Each person there must have felt already that the journey was worthwhile.

Syd Gregory was inching towards his century. Peel had

Reedman caught, but Charlie McLeod saw his little partner resist a long period of off-theory bowling with his score 99 before cutting to the boundary. There was no rash celebration: Gregory was under orders, and in any case he had made only 100 runs in 10 completed innings in Tests against England before this match.

At 400 McLeod's stumps were hit by Richardson, and Charlie Turner lasted only a quarter of an hour for a single before Peel had him caught behind by the grateful Gay. In came Blackham, the skipper, to bat cautiously. His sights must have been set on 600 at least.

Richardson and Peel, in one of the longest spells of bowling ever recorded, had operated all day until some time after lunch while 132 runs had been scored. The fast man's pace had slackened; he was bathing in sweat. The fielding wilted as spirits slumped and flesh protested. Gay, wretched man, dropped Gregory when he was 131. Then Blackham surprisingly received the benefit of a run-out appeal. Briggs and Ford took up the bowling, and in mid-afternoon the 500 was raised. The stand blistered on at two runs a minute until Australia's previous highest Test score – 551 at The Oval in 1884 – was passed.

Gregory hoisted Ford high out to Lancashire's Albert Ward when he was 194, but the catch was not held. From the next stroke Gregory had his double-century, and the lace parasols, handkerchiefs, and straw hats were waved in noisy delight. In the members' enclosure they collected £103 for him. The applause apparently lasted five minutes!

Stoddart himself got Gregory out – for 201, caught on the long-off boundary by Peel. The ninth-wicket stand of 154 between Gregory and Blackham remains an England–Australia record to this day.

Ernie Jones, Australia's muscular, uncouth fast bowler, came in as last man and smote all about him for a few minutes. Then Blackham, 74, having made his highest score in 62 Test innings, became victim of a six-inch break-back from Richardson (5 for 181 off 55.3 overs!) and England's misery was over at last. Australia were surely safe with 586 runs on the board.

Heavy cloud ominously blotted out the sun when England started batting, and by the end of the day the score stood at 130 for 3. Archie MacLaren fell early to Turner, Stoddart to Giffen, and J. T. Brown was run out after responding to Ward's call after a misfield. Ward was 67 not out, a courageous, determined knock.

His partnership of 71 with Brockwell was to be the best of the innings, and, but for Ford's 30, Briggs's game 57, and Gay's 33, England, batting on a pitch which had soaked up some unwelcome rain, would have fallen well short of their eventual 325 – an overawing deficit of 261. They followed on.

This time, though the outfield was thicker and consequently more difficult to penetrate, their resistance was more obstinate. The opening stand of 44 kindled real hope before MacLaren was deceived and bowled by Giffen's slower ball. During this innings Giffen, acting captain as Blackham's thumb had been split in the first innings, was to bowl 75 overs, taking 4 for 164. Not for the first time, critics asked if he might not have had an inflated opinion of his own ability as a bowler.

Now Stoddart joined Ward and added 71 precious runs before being caught at cover. When Brown and Ward then put on 102 for the third wicket, some of the preconceptions were blown away. Their magnificent bombardment took England within sight of Australia's mammoth total; continued resistance would mean Blackham's men being set some sort of target after all.

Ward was the first to fall, beaten by Giffen as he played back. His 117 remains one of the most valuable centuries ever made in Test cricket.

Jack Brown drove Giffen for four to reach his half-century, but with the total 245 – still 16 in arrears – he lofted the acting captain into the longfield and Ernie Jones, hurtling round at speed, brought off an astounding catch. England were perched indecisively with the four top men out.

Our smug latter-day advantage is that we may calmly examine every run and wicket wasted as destiny took its course. Peel, for example, was missed by Jones five yards from the bat and went on to be nine not out at the close. His partner, Brockwell, with so much depending on him, made 20 in the last drizzly overs. England were seven runs on with six wickets remaining.

Skies were still grey on Wednesday, but it was darker still in England, where no news had come through – and would not be coming through until the match was finished. The cable delay meant that an unbelieving British public received the story of the last three days in one eye-popping report.

Ernie Jones accounted for Brockwell with a 'bailer' and Peel, bowled off his foot, became Giffen's fourth victim: 296 for 6, a mere 35 ahead.

Little Briggs, who was to die seven years later in a Cheshire asylum, held his natural attacking instinct in check, and Ford ('Six foot-two of don't care') survived a chance and clubbed two fours in celebration. Briggs could restrain himself no longer, and he sailed into Giffen's medium-pace bowling, being dropped by the substitute fieldsman at square-leg. The score at lunch was 344 for 6; the lead now 83.

The crowd swelled further after the interval and saw the best of Ford. The tall, gangling Middlesex left-hander hit freely to all points of the driving compass and shared a priceless stand of 89 with Briggs before hitting a return catch to McLeod when two short of his 50.

Lockwood chipped in with an innings of 29, but meanwhile Briggs was lost when McLeod forced him to play on for 42. Eight gone for 398, and England's captain was observed clapping each run from the pavilion.

Gay raised the 400, then was bowled by Harry Trott for four, the only England batsman to fail to reach double-figures. With a solitary wicket remaining, England were 159 ahead. Tom Richardson, heavy with flu, flayed 12 useful runs, and when Lockwood was bowled, Australia were left to make 177 on a good, firm pitch. Would it be a 10-wicket or a nine-wicket win, asked the betting men.

At four o'clock Jack Lyons, the big hitter, and Harry Trott started the job, and in a quarter of an hour 25 runs were beside Lyons's name, a single to Trott. Stoddart placed three men near square on the leg side, and this seemed to disturb Lyons. Richardson put everything into it, and as in the first innings he got the ball through Lyons's defence and hit him a crunching blow on the knee. England had the piece of luck so important in close contests when the ball ricocheted into the stumps. It was Richardson's last gasp for the day; he retired at 32 for one wicket.

Giffen was circumspect and Trott 'ridiculously cramped', and as Australia seemed to be looking to the morrow, England grasped the chance to tighten the pressure. Peel beat Trott with his flight, and Gay pocketed the thin edge: 45 for 2. Darling got off his 'pair', but at 14 gave Stoddart a one-handed chance he couldn't hold. As rainclouds banked up Darling began hitting in all directions.

Giffen, the 'anchor-man', had been in for an hour and three-quarters for just 30 by the end of play, and his knee was tender after a blow from Lockwood's bowling. Darling had raced to 44, and with eight wickets in hand and only 64 now needed, Australia must have been everyone's heavy favourites.

The sixth day dawned in streaming sunshine. Giffen has recorded his delight at seeing the azure blue sky; yet only half the scene was visible: millions of raindrops had spattered the turf during the small hours. Somewhere the aboriginal rain-makers had exceeded the bounds of patriotic decency.

Blackham had feared rain all along, and now, his 'coffee-pot' face becoming forever part of Australian folklore, he lamented his team's likely fate with George Giffen as their drag left furrows in the soft ground in front of the team's hotel.

For once the Australians detested the sun's burning rays, feared their effect on the saturated pitch. The job would not be easy now. If only another 30 runs had been banked last evening.

For Stoddart's team, some of whom had spent the previous night drinking, thinking the match as good as lost, the task still lay ahead, though Peel and Briggs recognised well enough the favours awaiting them in the dark-stained pitch. Peel thought someone had watered it!

'Give me t'ball, Mr Stoddart', he said, 'and Ah'll get t'boogers out before loonch!' The extraction of five teeth just before the match no longer bothered him, and his skipper had sobered him up after his late-night indulgences by having him put under a cold shower.

An 11 o'clock start might have given Australia a chance, but when the cream-clad figures did eventually spill out into the sunlight the stickiness of the wicket was acute. (MacLaren recalled that Peel and Lockwood arrived late, having overslept, and it was only with Blackham's generous forbearance that the Englishmen took the field after the set time.)

Within 20 minutes the pitch was cut through and next to unplayable.

With only a few hundred people present, the Sydney Cricket Ground was like 'some silent cemetery' after the first five days of packed stands and cheering ranks. Richardson, bumping all over the place again, opened the bowling opposite Bobby Peel.

One kept low and Giffen edged it for four, and at the other end Joe Darling, realising the urgency of his mission, whacked Peel over the boundary for five (six would be awarded now, but then the batsmen had to change ends). At 130 Darling tried to repeat the shot, but Brockwell, in front of the two-and-sixpenny seats, clung to perhaps the most important catch of his career. Darling's 53 had been a gallant effort – in the manner of Neil Harvey's 92 not out, also at Sydney, 60 years later. In both cases the batsman's genius, if supported, could have won the day.

After Brown had badly missed Giffen, and with cabs and carriages streaming at the gallop across Moore Park as news of the tense situation spread, snub-nosed Briggs ceased licking his lips as he was put on in place of Richardson. In his first over Giffen slipped and was lbw for 41. That made it 135 for 4: 42 required.

Iredale did all he could against the leaping, creeping ball, and Gregory, with increased stature after his 201, stroked masterfully in spite of the increasing hazards. But Iredale mishit Briggs, who pouched the high return catch.

Reedman drove, and Gregory snicked and cut. The total groaned to 158 for 5. Only 19 runs and Australia would be home – on little Syd Gregory's back.

Alas, he edged Peel and Gay held the catch standing up. MacLaren suffered anguish in missing Reedman, but without further damage the South Australian jumped out desperately to Peel and was stumped. Eighteen to win, and three wickets remaining. 'Observer' observed Blackham pacing the balcony muttering 'Cruel luck!' over and over; Giffen standing stunned, singlet and shirt in hand; Graham, head in hands, a helpless twelfth man; Lyons sighing in vain now that his own vigorous innings was over.

Visualise the scene: Charlie Turner may be a champion bowler, Stoddart knows well enough; he can also bat, and a few well-timed blows from him would finish the match. The captain surveys the field. Turner makes two runs. Then he lifts a ball from Peel to cover point and Briggs secures the catch. Jones comes in, burly Jones the express bowler, who can bat only one way – brutally. He slams Briggs into the deepfield, and this time MacLaren holds it. Nine down for 162. Fifteen wanted. Jack Blackham, hand injured, walks to the centre and takes guard. The ball is sent up unerringly at the off stump. Accuracy is all. McLeod spars, takes a single; Blackham plays and winces at the pain. Stoddart peers anxiously. The bowlers, Peel and Briggs, Northcountrymen both, saunter to the crease, dispatch the ball, not daring to pitch even as close as middle stump. The ball spits away into Gay's gloves.

A single here and there, and Blackham wishes so fervently that he could use both hands firmly on the bat-handle. Peel in again: Blackham prods the ball back and it carries to Peel, who catches it safely! England have won!

They had won the match 'impossible to win'. No Test side before had ever won a match after having followed-on. It ended two minutes before lunch, and the final margin was 10 silly runs. Peel, the main hero of the hour, had 6 for 67 off 30 overs, Briggs 3 for 25 off 11.

England went on to win the second Test too, making 75 and 475 (Stoddart 173) and dismissing Australia for 123 and 333 (Richardson seven wickets, Peel five). Then Australia came back with crushing victories at Adelaide and Sydney, new boy Albert Trott announcing himself on to a brief and wondrous Test career with 8 for 43 in the third Test and 195 runs without being dismissed in his first three innings. Giffen and Turner took a lot of wickets and Iredale made 140 at Adelaide. Harry Graham, another to die in an asylum, made 105 at Sydney in his first Test innings on Australian soil, having made 107 at Lord's in his first Test, in 1893.

The stage was set for a classic match at Melbourne to decide the series, and the teams did not disappoint. More heroic bowling by Tom Richardson, another marathon from Giffen, hundreds by MacLaren and Brown for England, tall scores also from Gregory, Darling, Ward, Stoddart, and Peel. And at the end of it all, thanks predominantly to the miraculous last-day stand of 210 by Ward and Brown for the third wicket, England went on to win by six wickets.

It was a Test series fit to rank in terms of sustained tension and thrills with any in the 80 years since. And it all began with the Sydney turnabout just before Christmas 1894, when English stubbornness and fortitude, allied to the perversity of the Australian weather, led to a famous victory.

A. T.

THE CLOSEST TEST

Australia v West Indies, Brisbane,
December 1960

The previous Test match in Brisbane had been played at the dreariest pace. England and Australia batted at a rate of 130 runs a day, and Trevor Bailey took seven and a half hours over 68. The prospects this time were much healthier, with a West Indies touring side who were nothing if not entertaining, if also erratic; and there were two captains, Worrell and Benaud, who would surely not allow cricket to be played like trench warfare. On the eve of this first Test Sir Donald Bradman asked for a word with the Australian team. He spoke of the game's need of a re-awakening, he thought this could be the series to produce it, and he hoped that this Australian team could lead the way. It was up to the players themselves.

To be sure, the Test opened with a brilliant first day. The West Indies were 36 for 3 after the first hour; then at lunch, after another hour, 130 for 3. Garry Sobers was irresistible, playing an innings which was reckoned alongside any in Test cricket. It had been thought that Benaud was possibly his master, but it was Benaud especially who found that the best deliveries were punished equally – perhaps even harder – with the indifferent ones. To each ball, Sobers seemed to select the stroke he wanted: *defence* did not seem to be any part of that selection. With Sobers making 132 in three hours, and Worrell and Solomon adding 60s, West Indies reached 359 for 7 on that first day.

The second morning saw an innings of belligerence and high fun from Wes Hall, who smashed fast bowlers in the air and exasperated them further with ridiculously short singles. Meckiff with the third new ball was hit for 19 in an over – as many as in one pre-lunch session during the previous Brisbane Test. West Indies were all out for 453. They had got a lot of runs and quickly – so quickly that Worrell may not have been happy that Australia were able to start their reply before lunch on the second day, with the pitch at its best. He kept the game tight, rather than attacked, and with the leading Australian batsmen not in their best form the action was not quite as dashing as that which preceded it.

O'Neill survived chances and improved, after his century, to take his score up to 181. Of support which Favell, Mackay, and Davidson gave, Davidson's was the most handsome – indeed, the best of the Australian innings. Australia passed the West Indies total with only five wickets down, but then lost their last five in gaining a lead of 52.

On the fourth day the second West Indies innings started explosively. After an hour they were 75 for 1. But then Davidson proceeded to bowl them out, accounting for five of their first seven batsmen – including Sobers, who, to the bowler's manifest delight, was yorked for 14. By the early afternoon the West Indies realised they were facing defeat. Their situation worsened from a worrying to a desperate one, and after Worrell was out – again for 65 – Solomon batted 222 minutes for 47 and Alexander 67 minutes for five. To no avail, it seemed. At stumps they were 259 for 9, only 207 ahead. The game seemed as good as over. The unpredictable West Indies had set the match alight and now faded from it.

On the final morning Hall, again, and Valentine batted crucially for 40 minutes, adding 31 runs and leaving Australia to make 233 to win in 312 minutes. The last wicket fell when Hall, fittingly, was yorked by Davidson; it gave the left-armer six wickets for 87 in this innings and 11 wickets in the match. Already the game had seen memorable individual performances, and seen the initiative swing from one side to the other. Individuals were now to perform in such epic fashion as to make the game known as Hall's match or Davidson's match – but for the events which ultimately far transcended the individuals who contributed to them.

Australia's target of 233 represented a rate of 45 runs an hour. It was a pace which, if not brisk, would cause worry if it was pushed up by tight bowling or loss of wickets. Benaud had already shown a touch of unease in a protest against the batsman Hall running on the wicket.

It was Hall with the new ball – Hall who, as a fast bowler, should have found the pitch of least use on the last day – who now drove in two early blows to cause Australia real alarm. With one run on the board he had Simpson weakly fending off a lifting ball into short-leg's hands, and at seven he had Harvey snicking low into the slips where Sobers achieved that most improbable of feats, diving *forward* to hold a brilliant catch. To McDonald and O'Neill, Hall continued to give everything he had. Their task could be no more than survival, and at lunch Australia had struggled to a mere 28 for 2 after 70 minutes. The required rate had risen alarmingly from 45 runs-per-hour to 55.

After lunch, the batsmen resumed with new purpose. O'Neill took three fours and a three off Hall, for whom four overs cost 28 runs. Two of those fours, played within the same over, were the most polished of late cuts. Worrell posted no third man. O'Neill now went for the cut again, and edged to Alexander. Within a few balls McDonald, at the other end, was bowled by Worrell. Favell, who was all but bowled by Hall first ball, fell eight runs later in the leg trap. Australia were 57 for 5. Hall had taken four for 37. Calculations for run-rate were now forgotten, though in fact Australia needed 176 in 200 minutes from their last four wickets. In the battle for survival they had to keep taking runs, though; a positive attitude would at least cause Worrell some concern too, and lead to a loosening of the tight, attacking field. Mackay, who had repeatedly failed to pick up Hall's pace, must have been relieved to see the big man come off, perspiring and weary, to be replaced by Sobers and the spinners. Still runs were hard to come by. Davidson, again looking very sound, and Mackay had added 35 in an hour when Ramadhin turned a leg-break past Mackay's drive and bowled him. Australia were 92 for 6.

Benaud, not a great gatherer of runs in Test matches – though always a threat – started tentatively. He was almost bowled second ball and he continued uncertainly, even allowing for the shot which got him off the mark, a cleanly off-driven four against Valentine. At tea it was 110 for 6, and the required rate had inevitably now surpassed one-a-minute: it was 123 runs in 120 minutes. There seemed to be little realistic prospect of an Australian victory; but during the interval Sir Donald Bradman joined Benaud and Davidson in the players' tea-room. Bradman enthused about the quality of the contest throughout the five days and suggested that the match was building up to a fine climax. He asked if Benaud was going for a win or a draw, and was pleased to be told that it was a win.

Davidson on 16 and Benaud on six came out from tea determined to start by trying for all possible short singles, along with hitting any loose balls, before resorting to 'thrashing'. Pressuring the fielding side was a tactic which promised some success, as the West Indians had a history of letting excitement get to their nerves. That was what started to happen after tea. A rush of singles drew some wild fire at the stumps. This time, however, Caribbean excitement was steadied by a captain, Worrell, with the necessary experience and authority. Worrell also led by example, as he replaced Hall at the bowling crease. Hall had bowled just three overs and this time the battery was flat. So he was rested until, and in case, 200 was reached and a new ball became available. Davidson had twice hooked Hall gloriously, stepping inside the line and hitting off the full face of the bat. Against Worrell, Benaud immediately hit past mid-off for four. At the other end, Benaud hit Ramadhin over his head first-bounce into the fence – a stroke much more important to Benaud's confidence and to the fielding side's apprehension than the numerical value of four runs. Now Benaud was batting with great confidence, almost as well as Davidson – and Davidson was playing supremely well. Australia had at last gained in their struggle against the clock. With an hour remaining they wanted just under 60 runs, and with the batsmen approaching the 100 partnership and their own 50s, the balance had definitely swung towards Australia.

With Worrell continuing to gamble with Ramadhin, and Sobers' slower style, and with a four being struck almost every over, and the singles still being safely scampered, the 200 came up on cue. It was, it seemed, a welcome moment for Worrell. The Return of Hall was his last hope; more than that, it had begun to loom, almost, as a promise of salvation. As Hall took the new ball the score was 206 for 6. Exactly 30 minutes remained and Australia wanted 27 to win.

Immediately, Hall's run was again athletic, his action thunderous. Adrenalin had recharged the battery. The crowd, simmering with excitement, hushed to complete silence for the delivery of each ball, and then let out their breath with one voice: and something happened off every one of the eight balls in that over. There was a ball which Davidson flashed at and missed; there was one which he spiritedly hooked high to leg for four; there was another that was skied just out of reach of a catch; there was an absurdly short single off a ball played back very close to Hall; there was a frantic moment when Davidson and Benaud were both at the same end, with the ball coming in to that end, and the West Indies were unable to scramble it to the other end before Davidson got all the way back. For all the alarms, Australia added eight runs in the over. Hall's slump conveyed frustration and dejection.

Sobers now attempted to stem the rush. But he could not. The eight balls provided a leg-bye, three singles, a no-ball and a fiercely on-driven four by Benaud. Nine more runs had taken the total to 223 for 6. Only 10 needed in 15 minutes – in probably three more overs, perhaps four. The game was as good as over.

Hall again, hardly even the Last Hope now. Still, the over was splendidly bowled. Benaud sparred more than once without getting a touch, and just jammed down to stop the best of yorkers. Only a dashed single – one run only – came off the over. Hall had at least managed to keep the pressure on, with nine runs now needed in 10 minutes.

Sobers again. Two quick singles made it 226 for 6. Just seven runs needed. One of the singles was taken close to Solomon at short square-leg, who might have been quicker to seize on it. Now, as the ball was again played to Solomon's side, he moved as quickly as the batsmen did. The non-striker Davidson, even with his backing-up, had no chance. He was yards out as Solomon's throw hit the stumps, and would have been out anyway even if 'keeper Alexander had been required to complete the run-out. The batsmen's success between the wickets had encouraged them to take one short single too many; this was a bad one.

With Australia 226 for 7 and stormy applause welcoming back Davidson after his great innings of 80, wicket-keeper Grout hurried in. Time had become crucial again, Australia still needing seven runs with four balls of this over left and, if necessary, one over after that – from Hall. Grout could not score from either of his first two balls. Should he now try for a single, and risk having to face Hall? No single could be ignored in this situation, and one was taken off the seventh ball. Benaud, of course, would now look for one off his last ball. Sobers also knew it, and so did the fieldsmen, all of them head down, feet moving, ready to pounce. Sobers has possibly never delivered a more important ball. It was a length which Benaud could not force through the swiftly converging field.

So, at four minutes to six, began the last over. Australia needed six to win, with three wickets in hand. Many of the spectators at the Gabba had now left their seats on the banking and come to stand at the pickets. All over Australia motorists driving home were pulling their cars over to the roadside to hear out the disconcerting radio commentary...

Hall steadied himself at the end of his run. His target was Grout's wicket. He sucked in his breath and was away, with strong, elastic strides: like some mighty locomotive, a giant of the iron road. Grout, caught as in the headlights, was struck around the groin. The ball dropped to the pitch, and Grout was about to drop too – when he saw Benaud charging at him for the single. Forced to run for his life, Grout struggled to the the other end.

Now Hall was faced with Benaud. Although he had been told by his captain to abandon the bumper he now elected to risk another. Benaud shaped for the hook; the ball flicked his gloves and went on through to a jubilant Alexander. Benaud was out for 52, as Hall took his fifth wicket for 61. Australia were 228 for 8, needing five runs in six balls – now from the pure tail-enders.

Ian Meckiff walked in slowly. Time now was irrelevant. His first ball from Hall was not a bouncer. It was a length ball, finding the middle of Meckiff's anxious bat, allowing no run. Five runs needed off five balls. Grout now knew that big hits and snicks could not be counted on. At least a single had to be attempted off every ball – even at the risk of a run-out, with two wickets left. As Hall bowled again to Meckiff, Grout was moving. As he saw the ball passing wide down the leg side he set off, calling Meckiff. Alexander, standing back, could not defeat Grout's dash; instead he threw the ball to Hall who had followed far through, and Hall turned and hurled at the stumps to which Meckiff was heading. He missed. Valentine flung himself at the ball to save the over-throws. One more run to Australia, 229 for 8. Four to win off four balls.

Hall bowled now to Grout. The batsman swung, he mis-hit, the ball lobbed up into the mid-wicket area. Kanhai was under it, safe hands ready – when Hall's mad figure crashed into and over him, grabbing for the catch, and knocking the ball to the ground. The word was Preposterous. No one could believe what they were watching: not the half-crazed spectators, not the stunned West Indian fieldsmen, not the Australians who were watching in a deranged state on their dressing-room patio. Perhaps to Grout and Meckiff, though, the moment had some reality: in the pandemonium they had taken a single. Australia were 230 for 8, now needing three runs from three balls.

Hall went back again to his mark, a shamed figure. At least he still had a purpose; he had a chance to make up for his madness. This next ball was again fast, on a good length, straight. And this time Meckiff, also, had decided to swing. It was a cross-batted shot but it connected. The ball soared away splendidly towards the mid-wicket boundary. It seemed a certain four, but Hunte was pursuing it furiously to where in fact it stopped in the un-cut clover of the outfield. In any case Meckiff and Grout were making sure by sprinting between the wickets. They had taken two and were turning again, when Hunte picked up. The third run would win the match. From 80 or 90 yards away, Hunte's throw was as long, as low, as fast, and as straight as it had to be – and as Grout dived full-length for the line Alexander's gloves had swept the stumps over. The shout was mighty and umpire Hoy's finger was up.

The game was tied with Australia on 232 for 9. But two balls still remained. After this fantasy, surely whatever happened now would be anti-climax? Last man Lindsay Kline faced Hall; the fieldsmen crouched to stop the single; Meckiff at the other end prepared to go for it. The ball pitched middle-and-leg, Kline's bat made contact, the ball ran away towards square-leg – to the left hand of Solomon. The batsmen were under way and flying as Solomon picked up one-handed, cleanly. There was no one yet up at the wickets as Solomon threw, with one stump to aim at . . . It was also the script-writer's final throw. The bails went flying, with Meckiff still at the stretch and short, and into the air like dervishes went the West Indian fieldsmen.

There was pandemonium everywhere. When it had finally eased in the Press Box, the result which at first was given variously as a win, a loss, and a draw, was agreed as a tie – the first in the history of Test cricket. At the end, Benaud had gone out on to the field to welcome Worrell in, and now the players drank together all evening. Sir Donald was there too. Having hoped, and asked, for cricket which would breathe new life into the game, he surely was justified in describing the result as 'The greatest Test of all time'.

N. H.

A LITTLE HATRED HELPS

Australia v England, Sydney, December 1954

When England, under Len Hutton's tight leadership, won the Ashes from Australia in 1953, 19 years after losing them in 1934, the joy was unconfined and longlasting. Only in the fifteenth Test against Australia after the war did England manage to win, when Freddie Brown's side won the fifth Test at Melbourne in the 1950–51 series. That 'elusive victory' did more than prevent a five-nil whitewash to Australia: it showed that they could be beaten, that England were taking shape as a true Test team again. There had been close matches at the start of the 1950–51 rubber, but Australia triumphed each time, adding weight to the theory that even with the great Bradman retired they were next to invincible. The Melbourne victory set up the distinct possibility that the following series in England in 1953 might go England's way.

By means of weather interference, heroic defiance, and negative, spoiling tactics England drew the first four Tests of that 'Coronation series'; then came the sweet, almost tear-jerking, triumph at The Oval: an eight-wicket win set up chiefly by Hutton, Edrich, May, Bailey, Bedser, Trueman, Laker, and Lock. Twelve months later came the task of defending those Ashes in Australia. The team, with Hutton again at the helm, set out with reasonable confidence.

By 1 December 1954 they were practically on their knees. Hutton, with certain respectable motives, put Australia in to bat at Brisbane and fielded through all kinds of mortifications until Ian Johnson's men had made 601, declaring with eight wickets down. Catches were dropped, Morris and Harvey made big centuries, and the England bowling figures made macabre reading: Bedser 1 for 131, Statham 2 for 123, Bailey 3 for 140, and the fourth fast/fast-medium bowler Tyson 1 for 160.

Who was Tyson? He was Lancashire-born, educated at

Durham University, rejected by his native county, and given an opportunity by Northamptonshire. He was no mere fast bowler. He bowled at such a pace that batsmen stiffened upon first facing him, for here was someone who propelled the ball at a speed never encountered by them before. He took an extremely long run, and at the climax of his approach to the crease he bent his mighty back many degrees in reverse before plunging his enormous shoulders into a heaving, power-packed delivery, following through with the force of the recoil of a long-distance cannon.

Word soon spread. He stunned the touring Indians in 1952, battered a few Australian ribs and thighs in 1953, and was given his first England cap in 1954 against Pakistan, who surprisingly beat England at The Oval for the first time. Tyson took 4 for 35 and 1 for 22, and was soon on his way to Australia, where his name meant hardly anything to anyone.

After Brisbane it represented something akin to futility. One wicket for 160 runs off 29 eight-ball overs, bowled off a run starting somewhere out near the sightscreen!

Defeat by an innings and 154 runs sent England to Sydney, via the Victoria match at Melbourne, in apprehensive mind. Peter May had made a century against Victoria, and the balding fast bowler, trying a shorter run-up, took 6 for 68, having Colin McDonald caught behind by Evans, and bowling the other five, who included Neil Harvey, Australia's dapper, high-scoring left-hander, and Ian Johnson. Tyson looked a much more impressive bowler all of a sudden, keeping a fuller length, maintaining his speed, and showing every sign of improved stamina – the outcome of eliminating a mile or two from his cumulative run-up!

Hutton and his co-selectors stuck by Tyson for the second Test, to be played at Sydney. The shock came when it was known that the lionhearted Alec Bedser was dropped. He had carried England's bowling almost singlehanded on his expansive shoulders ever since 1946, but shingles contracted in Perth had diminished his sting as a fast-medium bowler and the captain was now prepared to put all his faith in the raw speed of Tyson and the tirelessness of Statham, backed by the clever fast-medium bowling of Trevor Bailey, the medium-pace off-spin and floaters of Appleyard, and Wardle's left-arm spin. Arthur Morris, standing in as captain for the injured Johnson, won the toss for Australia and put England in to bat.

Hutton took Bailey in with him to open the innings, an

experiment which seemed to be working when the number two was still with his skipper after half an hour, though still scoreless. Hutton had, on the whole, protected him from the menace of Lindwall, who was varying his speed beautifully and bending the ball late in either direction. At last, though, he had a clear sight of Bailey and knocked his middle stump out.

When May was caught off Archer, who took the new ball in place of the injured Miller, England were 19 for two wickets. That was grim enough in the close and cloudy afternoon, but when Hutton went to a stupendous diving catch by Davidson at leg-slip England were in a spin. That was always the effect of Hutton's dismissal. He was almost everything to England's batting. So long as he survived, all was not lost. He had played the guileful Lindwall and hostile Archer suspiciously, skilfully, and successfully, unleashing one memorable back-cut off a short ball from Lindwall that skidded to the boundary at the base of the Hill almost faster than the eye could follow. Now he was out, and soon Graveney followed him. Edrich popped up a catch to gully off a kicker, and Tyson was bowled by Lindwall for a duck. Evans was caught at the wicket, Cowdrey, 23, met the same fate, and Appleyard was taken at slip by Hole off Davidson. England 111 for 9, and Australians, some perhaps with the semblance of a yawn, envisaging going to the third Test two-up already.

The final wicket was sustained by Johnny Wardle, a clowning, free-swinging left-hander, and Brian Statham, hardly more elegant, also a left-hander with the bat, Yorkshire and Lancashire sharing a desperate cause. They added 43 unspeakably welcome runs with some outrageous 'strokes', and England's total was dragged up to 154, well under half what they must have hoped for.

That evening, Morris was caught at leg-slip by Hutton off Bailey, which was something to comfort the visitors, and Australia ended at 18 for one.

On the Saturday England came back into the game, with every run scored, missed, conceded, or saved carrying immense significance. Favell and Burke carried Australia to 65 before Favell was caught by Graveney at second slip off Bailey, who was bowling on an admirable line around the off stump. No sooner had the hundred come up after lunch than Burke fell the same way for 44.

Harvey, the danger-man, batted for over an hour before becoming Tyson's first victim of the match – caught in the gully off a vicious lifter just as it seemed he might be launching into better things. Tyson's direction and length had left much to be desired earlier, but he was settling down now, and took the inspiration from Harvey's downfall that any bowler would recognise. Statham's accuracy and stamina were, as always, marvelled at by all involved in the action, and most of the great crowd and press observers. The match was turning into a titanic struggle.

Graeme Hole was next to go, yorked all over the place by Tyson, whose speed was too much for the tall man's high back-swing. Benaud made 20 runs with as many close escapes. That was 141 for 6, still 13 behind.

Two youngsters, Ron Archer and Alan Davidson, the most outstanding of the large array of all-rounders to be found in Australian cricket at that time, swung things back Australia's way – and did it by boldness. Archer put Australia ahead with a six over long-on off Appleyard, and, in an hour, 52 were added in the course of slashes, misses, thumping drives, and edges. The new ball put paid to the recovery: Statham knocked Davidson's leg stump back, and Archer, top scorer with 49, was caught at third slip by Hutton off Tyson. Lindwall made a useful 19 before being caught behind swinging at a bouncer from Tyson. That ball was to have repercussions.

This left the last pair at the wicket, and it was in England's interests to keep them there for a while in order to avoid an awkward few minutes' batting that evening. The bowlers did their job, bowling wide, and Australia did not declare, neither did a batsman throw his wicket away. Tyson had four wickets, and could presumably have taken a fifth without much difficulty, but when just 10 minutes remained, it was the signal to 'move in', and Bailey, whose efforts early in the innings had struck the first cracks in Australia's foundations, polished the innings off by bowling Langley. Australia all out for 228, a lead of 74; two days gone – days of tension and fascination.

Bailey again opened the innings with Hutton, and again allowed the bowler to do as he liked, meeting everything with a resolute bat – even half-volleys. After almost 40 minutes he touched one to Langley and was out for six – 18 for 1.

May began confidently and his captain responded. Boundaries came, and the sun showed through at last. A short ball from Archer was met by a virile cross-bat from the tall, powerful May and dispatched through mid-wicket. Hutton glanced elegantly for four, took four more for his classical, distinctive

Andrew Stoddart, England's leader in the extraordinary Test match against Australia in 1894 which was won by only 10 runs on the sixth day. *Photo David Frith*

Edwin Boaler Alletson. *Photo Nottingham Evening Post*

The Hon. Lionel Tennyson, who led Hampshire in a topsy-turvy match against Warwickshire in 1922 seen here with Warwick Armstrong. *Photo Press Association*

Stan McCabe (left), creator of three of cricket's greatest Test innings, ready for action with the redoubtable Don Bradman. *Photo Central Press*

Another wicket to Laker: Ian Craig lbw during Australia's first innings, Old Trafford 1956. *Photo Sport & General*

McKenzie is caught by Brown off Underwood and England are within sight of a thrilling victory at The Oval in 1968. *Photo Central Press*

Snow caught-and-bowled Chandrasekhar 0 – and England's collapse against India at The Oval continues. The tourists went on to their first ever victory in England. *Photo Central Press*

A square-cut to the boundary and Glenn Turner has his thousand runs in May 1973. *Photo Patrick Eagar*

cover-drive, and played Archer uppishly through short-leg for yet another boundary. Soon the deficit would be wiped off.

Then the game was turned upside-down again. Johnston, the lanky, laughing, left-arm medium-pacer, bowled a wider ball into the breeze, Hutton stretched for it as if to play his smooth and deceptively powerful square-drive, checked the stroke, and slightly lifted it to gully, where Benaud clutched the catch. Three balls later Tom Graveney played at a ball going across him (Johnston was bowling over the wicket) and edged it to Langley. England 55 for 3, still 19 behind. Over lunch there was speculation as to what time the match would finish.

May and Cowdrey – one about to turn 25, the other four days away from his 22nd birthday – were England's premier batting hopes. May had made his name at Cambridge, Cowdrey at Oxford, both after distinguished school performances. Now, someone jested, Cambridge and Oxford were in the same boat. Most felt that the vessel was sinking fast.

But the young men baled the boat out and, in comforting sunshine, increased the stroke-rate, while always maintaining a strict vigilance. May's driving caught the eye, as did his cutting of anything short. Crisply and with a sense of command he struck the ball away in a cultured yet clinical manner, reducing to a simple exercise what on the opening day had seemed preposterously difficult. Cowdrey, as the world was to discover in the 20 years to follow, could be all ease and grace, steering the ball between fieldsmen to the fence without apparently exerting himself in the slightest, then falling into a period of impotence, when all manner of delivery seemed to freeze him into anxious circumspection.

May, with that curious on-side grip of the bat, tortured the leg-side field, cracking balls on the stumps through mid-on, through mid-wicket, past square-leg. The fast bowlers seemed less fast and the ball seemed to be moving in a more honest line from bowler's hand to bat. Benaud, the young leg-spinner, came on at 118 to begin a spell of 17 overs spanning the tea interval, and with a cordon of superb fielders on the off-side run-making was anything but easy. The slightest mistiming would result in a catch to Harvey, with Burke or Favell patrolling the cover field. Benaud's accuracy was remarkable. Time and again the ball curled from the bat and described an arc to backward point, the batsmen contemplating a swift single but returning to their creases.

They added 116 for the fourth wicket in over three hours,

Cowdrey, having just passed his 50, eventually lofting Benaud out to Archer at long-off, where the catch was taken with ease. Bill Edrich, the small, doughty Middlesex all-rounder renowned for his courage and now in his thirty-ninth year, came to see May through the final 20-odd minutes. During that time he saw the ball to hit, and hit it, taking four with a hook off Johnston, followed by another four off-driven, and a shotgun pull to the fence from a short ball by Benaud. May reached the boundary again with masterly drives, and 33 were added, taking England to 204 for 4 at the close, May 98. The new ball would be taken in the morning.

The fourth day began to the accompaniment of light drizzle, and the new ball was not taken immediately. May reached his century, his first against Australia, and was bowled by Lindwall without further ado, the in-swinger doing its work and ensuring that England were in no position to race away to an impossible total.

Tyson came in. He was 'on a pair'. Soon he was off it. And soon he was flat on his back, unconscious. It happened when Lindwall dropped one short (it will be remembered that Tyson dismissed him with a bouncer) and he could only turn his back on it, ostrich-like, being in no position to duck. The smack was resounding, sickening. He crumpled to the turf like a shot bull, lifted his head in a spasm that promised recovery, then slumped back quite still. The players ran to him and two ambulance men ran from the pavilion, and it was fully five minutes before he was assisted, very dazed, from the field, the lump on the back of his head visible from a hundred yards. It seemed likely that he would not be seen again in the match.

The perky Evans came in – not a happy situation, rather like driving on after an unsightly road accident – but Lindwall, unnerved by the incident, was not to repeat himself. Evans, playing some distance from his body, was missed by Hole at slip first ball, and it seemed England would go to lunch without further disturbance and with time to collect themselves. Then, just as the salads were being set on the tables, Edrich played on to Archer for 29 and England, 232 for 6, were 158 ahead. Touch and go.

Evans was soon caught after the interval and when everyone expected to see Wardle emerge from the pavilion, out came Tyson. He was still feeling groggy, but the X-ray had shown no cracks in his skull, and he was ready to do his bit once again. The crowd greeted him with warmth, but he was not to stay long. After a loudly-cheered four through extra-cover off Johnston and another straight off Archer he was bowled by Lindwall, for nine.

Wardle could have done nothing better for England than to have repeated his first innings 35, but this time he could manage only eight before Lindwall claimed him lbw as his third wicket. That left England's last pair together: Statham and Appleyard.

The last five wickets had fallen for 28 runs, slanting the odds fairly positively into Australia's favour; but this last stand became worth 46, and put a sterner expression on the faces of Australia's batsmen. Hereabouts, Morris came in for criticism by sticking to his faster bowlers. Lindwall and Davidson were both eventually rested, but Appleyard's angled straight bat and Statham's shrewd application of defence and rustic attack had mischievously raised the total close to 300. They were only four short when Johnston, having tossed a few into the air, found the edge of Statham's bat and Langley did the rest. Australia needed 223, and it was 20 minutes past three when Statham, pads proudly removed, began the bowling – into the wind, as was so often his lot.

There was drama aplenty in that first over, though no wicket for England. Favell was rapped on the pads playing back; Edrich couldn't hold another ball as it was edged high above him; two balls later Favell was within an inch of being bowled; then he put a ball involuntarily to the long-leg fence. Tyson measured out his run.

He bowled at a rare pace from the start, particularly so if his earlier knockout be considered. Evans, keeping wicket, was leaping into the air to take him well on the way to the sight-screen. Yet Morris calmly steered a full toss between second and third slips, the ball cracking into the fence at third man like a musket shot. Then he waved his bat airily at a couple of shorter deliveries and looked suddenly frail and fallible. At the other end he tried to hook Statham, the ball kept lower than anticipated, and he was lbw. One down for 27.

After tea, in the first over from Tyson, Favell edged one to slip, where Edrich this time held on with both hands. Two for 34. When Harvey played and missed at the first two balls he received, there were gasps all round. Australia were struggling now. England, plodding uphill since the first ball of the match, were at last on more level ground.

Burke and Harvey, both scorers of centuries in their initial Tests against England, held on for all they were worth. Hutton, aware that his attacks had to be timed to a nicety, rested

Tyson and Statham and brought on Appleyard and Bailey, who continued to pin the batsmen down. Then Wardle came on with his teasing spin, compelling Burke to regard each ball as a potential hand grenade. He played two maiden overs.

The speed twins were called up again, but the third breakthrough did not come, and Wardle bowled the final over of the day as the shadows enveloped the square. Harvey slammed him for two boundaries, reminding England of how vain their hopes of victory would be if he should get settled in on the final day.

That final day began with Australia 72 for 2, Harvey (26) having added 38 so far with Burke in 78 minutes.

The attendance was low, as it usually is on the final day of a Test match, though goodness knows this is often the time for the greatest drama of all. Yet 135,350 passed through the turnstiles for this match, which as a contest never for a moment lost its edge or gave a single spectator cause to regret his effort and outlay in coming to the ground.

On the final morning little time was lost in chalking up the next piece of excitement. In his second over Tyson burst through Burke's dour defence and battered the base of the stumps. Four balls later in the same over he whistled one through Hole and displaced his middle stump. It was the second time in the match that the tall blond batsman had been beaten by sheer speed.

Australia were now 77 for 4 as Benaud joined Harvey. Tyson, breathing easily, showed no sign of slackening his fiery pace.

Harvey, small and compact, seemed in no real trouble, though he was continually forced back by Tyson's lift from the straw-coloured pitch. Benaud seemed in reasonable comfort. The hundred came, and Hutton relieved Statham with Appleyard. He came close to bowling Benaud with his first ball, which turned between bat and pad. Appleyard continued to use the air cunningly, and shortly Benaud was tempted into lunging meatily at one which hung in its flight, and the ball climbed until it was a speck in the sky before plunging in anything but a direct descent towards square-leg. Tyson waited for it anxiously, adjusting his feet as the ball grew larger and swirled earthwards. Stretching at the last split-second, he clutched the ball and his team-mates ran to him in delight.

Archer came in, and at lunch Australia had made 118 for the loss of five men, only 46 runs having been squeezed out of a tense hour and a half. A number of Sydney businessmen left their offices at lunchtime and didn't appear again that day.

The next blow for England was struck by Tyson, now established as a demon, the name on everyone's lips. He brought one back from outside the off stump and Archer could only help it into his stumps: 122 for 6.

Still Harvey was held in captivity, the infielders stopping singles towards the end of most overs. Davidson, also a left-hander, had to face the music, which was now reaching a regular crescendo. After making five, he edged Statham off the splice, and Godfrey Evans launched himself horizontally to catch the ball two-handed in front of the slips. Again it was the Evans uplift, creating excitement right through the team. 'Bring on the next batsman!' the bowlers might have been shouting.

Lindwall came in and bustled eight runs off the remainder of the over. He had made a century in a Test against England eight years before, and needed to be prised out before he could get Australia up to requirement. Tyson began to bowl to him, with the general expectation being that he might let loose something short and hair-raising. Two balls were enough: both well up to the bat, the first jagging in towards the stumps, the second crashing into them before Lindwall had sighted it.

Wicket-keeper Langley, tenth man in, saw nine runs added, none by him, before a Statham in-swinger bowled him off-stump. That was nine down for 145 – still 78 short of victory – and it was only half-past two. Last man Bill Johnston, gangling, aptly placed in the batting order, came in alongside the umpire, who had gone to fetch a replacement stump, the force of Statham's last ball having snapped the old one off at the base. Johnston was almost bowled by his first ball and close to lbw to the second. The formalities were almost over ... except that Harvey, now 64, having been kept in near-submission and a state of starvation, began to punch everything within reach. His previous partners had let him down in some of the strokes they had played and in their poor reading of the game. Harvey, of the keen eye, nimble feet, strong wrists, and cool nerve, could have got them home – but in adult cricket the last man doesn't carry on. Johnston, his last partner, held on, sometimes flicking balls with an ungainly, one-handed swish down to long-leg, sometimes playing and missing. He scampered twos when they were required, even threes, stood stock still when long, easy singles were sacrificed in the interests of shielding him.

Bailey replaced Statham, and Harvey drove him back over his head for four, having hooked Tyson to the pickets with ominous certainty. Tyson now showed signs of fatigue. England's captain was grim-faced.

Harvey moved through the 80s, and, having driven Bailey beautifully 'on the up', reached 92. It would have been a century had all the refused singles been taken. Hutton decided to give Tyson another over, with Johnston taking strike. Three years before, he and Ring had brought off a sensational one-wicket victory over West Indies at Melbourne by adding 38 for the final wicket as the fielding side showed every evidence of panic.

Again Tyson bowled somewhat tiredly outside-leg, and Johnston jabbed at it and got four to long-leg. Thirty-nine now added; 39 further wanted. The next ball passed by his hip; he failed to touch it. Again, a leg-side delivery, and this time he did get a touch, and Evans caught it joyously to give Tyson his tenth wicket in the match, and England a precious victory by 38 runs to get on even terms. Hutton and his men had a very merry Christmas.

Tyson, with figures of 4 for 45 and 6 for 85 off his 31.4 eight-ball overs, considered this the best game of cricket in which he ever played. After being floored by Lindwall, he 'was so sore that I swore they would not win', and he quoted Lindwall as saying that had he not flattened Tyson, Australia would have won the series.

As it was, England won the New Year Test at Melbourne by 128 runs after Tyson had demolished Australia in their second innings for 111, taking 7 for 27 on a broken pitch. The Ashes were made safe at Adelaide with a five-wicket win, and Australia managed a draw in the rain-ruined fifth Test, back at Sydney. In the series Frank Tyson, the 'Typhoon', took 28 wickets at 20.82 and his gallant major partner, Brian Statham, took 18 at 27.72. It was one of the heaviest drubbings ever handed out to Australia, yet after the débâcle of the first Test, at Brisbane, the odds against it must have been longer than Tyson's original run-up.

He was 24. It seemed he would be England's spearhead for years to come. But the success was never to be repeated on such a scale. Eventually he moved to Melbourne, having married an Australian, and became a popular and incisive cricket commentator, repeating the strange migration of Harold Larwood into the midst of the people he had tormented when an England fast bowler in 1933.

'A little hatred helps', Tyson once wrote in assessing the attitude necessary in a successful fast bowler, though he was the pleasantest of company, and was accepted into the world of those he once conquered with a warmth and readiness peculiar to Australians.

A. T.

EVERYONE'S TEST

England v West Indies, Lord's, June 1963

It might have been Wes Hall's match; it might have been Fred Trueman's match; it might have been Dexter's or Close's match, or Basil Butcher's. But, like the tied Test in Brisbane, the parts simply contributed to the whole, to a great Test match. Indeed, if it was anyone's match, it possibly belonged to the West Indies spectators who each day filled the Nursery end at Lord's where, for no extra charge, they could look down the line of the wicket like true experts and loudly offer encouragement and comment. It was not always so. Those who had once seen themselves as poor cousins in a foreign land were now discovering the confidence to express themselves as folk did back in the Caribbean; and sober dark suits and white shirts were beginning to give way to the freer attire of Shaftesbury Avenue. By collectively putting a little more velocity into each delivery of Wes Hall, and helping to dig out any scuttling delivery which threatened a vital stand, they provided such a communion with the play as is so necessary in the theatre, and which Lord's had perhaps never experienced in so volatile a manner.

It began when Trueman, with smooth action and menace, bowled the first over of the match and Hunte – continuing where he left off from his 182 at Manchester – hit each of the first three balls for four. These were the first shots in a conflict which, quite remarkably, was to be conducted almost throughout between fast bowlers on one hand and militant batsmen on the other. At best, the conflict was to be of Wagnerian intensity. The play was never to lapse into dullness. And the advantage was to shift constantly – more often, though less decisively, than in Brisbane's tied Test.

The first day was in fact the quietest of the five, though tense. At Old Trafford one of the most exciting batting sides in the world had mauled England for 501; but throughout this day their application was as untypical as it was admirable. Day-long they scored at less than two and a half runs an over while, under a grey sky, Shackleton and Trueman together bowled 70 out of 108 overs. When, at the end of the day, Trueman and Shackleton returned to take the new ball, they again controlled the play. Trueman, crucially, had Kanhai playing to the on as the ball cut across, edging to gully; and then punctured Worrell's statesman-like calm, as he caught the captain wrong-footed and sheared the bails. The day ended with the West Indies 245 for 6: not a commanding score by any means, but one which in the conditions promised to look healthy enough before the match was much older.

Under fine skies, a capacity crowd of 30,000 swarmed into Lord's for the Friday's play. This day there was richer excitement, and one of the most memorable of all Test innings. The entertainment began with the entry of Wes Hall as a batsman, to delight all the crowd with a performance suggestive of both a knight at joust and a clown. When he connected, the crowd down at J stand rose as one to shout and sing; when he clamped down on the next ball, they shouted, with one voice, 'NNOH!' – No, not a show! For the England players the joke soon wore thin; and Trueman must with difficulty have restrained himself from bowling the bouncer even at a bowler as least as fast as himself. In the end there was no need. Hall was left 25 not out as, in the twinkling of an eye, Shackleton took the last three wickets, a belated reward for bowling 50 overs for less than 100 runs. Trueman meanwhile had bowled 44 overs for 100 runs and six wickets, had performed like the great bowler he was, and could easily have taken those six wickets twice over. Noble performances, these, but the fact was that West Indies had put 301 runs on the board: and England now had to go in and face Hall and Griffith on a wicket that was still offering some assistance to bowlers. Micky Stewart and John Edrich, flinty Surrey men though they both were, and tenacious as they had been at Manchester, seemed to the most fearful of English minds to be as Christians before the lions. One observer saw Hall and Griffith, the fastest and most hostile bowlers in the world, as 'assassins'; another wrote of expecting one or other opening batsman to be 'struck by lightning' in the 25 minutes to lunch.

Indeed it started just as badly as England feared. To the first ball he faced, Edrich was caught down the leg side, and in the last over before lunch Stewart was caught in the slips off his gloves. Both bowlers were fast and menacing, though this time the more dangerous of them seemed to be Griffith. England could clutch only a little comfort from the fact that Dexter had started with resolution, collecting 16 mostly forthright runs in the short period to lunch – though in that last over which accounted for Stewart, the most hostile over Griffith had bowled, he was fortunate to jab the ball from the inside edge, past the leg stump, for four.

After the interval, accompanied by Barrington, Dexter came out to play an innings which was to cause eternal regret for those who lingered over their luncheon. He stood bare-headed, hair trimmed close, less like his Down Under image of Lord Ted than that of a guardsman at play or the hero of some boys' story. The mood was on him, and he started against Griffith by answering fire with fire. Griffith thundered down from the pavilion end, with dark brick background, and twice in an over Dexter counter-drove explosively, the ball making a loud report off the bat as it went to the long-off fence. Against such speed he was playing with his front foot classically advanced, the bat coming through in a full arc and finishing over his head. Soon enough, Griffith dropped short; Dexter's bat met the ball at the right-angle and sent it square into the Tavern pickets. Came the yorker, and the bat descending from its full pickup impacted the ball out and away down the wicket, past the bowler's feet, for three runs. Hall likewise was despatched to mid-wicket, was square-cut and late-cut. Meanwhile, Barrington continued to take a minimal amount of the bowling, appeared hasty and anxious when he did have to face, making the fast bowlers once again look like giants. Urged on by an excited crowd, the giants sought more thunder against Dexter, Dexter thundered back, whirlwind met whirlwind; the rest of the players were made to seem – and perhaps felt – almost out of place.

Dexter had gone past 50; Griffith and Hall, when their walk back to the mark grew visibly jaded, were taken out of the attack. Sobers came on and was greeted with a four through cover, but with Gibbs managed to reduce the scoring rate. Sobers soon changed ends and now the left-armer's angle, after troubling Dexter, caught him lbw playing slightly across the line.

In just an hour since lunch the score had gone from 20 to 102. Dexter in all had made 70 out of 100 in 80 minutes. Other dashing innings could be instanced in Test cricket, but perhaps none with the circumstances so fraught, against bowling so hostile, none which seemed so to overturn the pattern of the play.

The pavilion received Dexter like Rome welcoming home a centurion. But in this case the battle was far from won; and straightaway the England innings, and the character of the match, reverted to type. Cowdrey was soon bowled as he played a half-heartedly ambitious stroke at Gibbs, and it was left to Barrington to marshal England's continuing challenge. At the end of the day, though, with Barrington and Parks both out, England were slightly at a disadvantage at 244 for 7. No recognised batsman remained, and in the morning the new ball would soon be due.

In the morning, in fact, the West Indies initiative was all but annulled by a most perky Titmus, who continually jumped across his stumps to turn the ball through the on side, kept snatching short singles, and by the end was farming the bowling like a veteran. At the fall of each of the last England wickets, J stand erupted as if activated by an electric charge; and when Titmus got his 50 the rest of the crowd responded as for Victory Day. Lord's was packed to the corners for its famous Saturday, and the day was to prove no disappointment. England finally finished only four short at 297. They had scored their runs an hour faster than had their opponents, at 48.5 per 100 balls compared with 37.6. Not now could the West Indians be characterised as 'ebullient' and the Englishmen as 'stolid'. Both sides were as equals, and were to remain so as the finely-balanced match continued.

The West Indies now had a half-hour's batting to lunch, just as England had the previous day. There was more spectacular action now, with Hunte hooking Trueman for six and then being dropped off a difficult chance into the slips, but the end result was just as disastrous: Cowdrey swooped from short second slip to take Hunte off Shackleton and then, amid renewed uproar, smoothly caught and tossed aloft an edge from McMorris off Trueman. At lunch the West Indies were 15 for 2. So, it was decisively England's morning – though not yet, not by any means, decisively their day or their match.

Trueman and Shackleton continued after lunch. Kanhai was serious and resolute, his head low, his bat straight. He ignored his spectacular shots. He played three successive maidens from Titmus. England's fieldsmen, as keen as hounds, dived for technical half chances. It appeared that no wicket was going to come easily, when Kanhai steered Shackleton straight into Cowdrey's midriff. Acting captain on this day, with Dexter nursing a troublesome knee, Cowdrey had caught batsmen one, two, and three. He had three catches also in the first innings, and no culpable misses; the runs he did not contribute here or at Manchester were being well compensated.

With the West Indies 64 for 3 all attention now focused on the new batsman, Sobers. Trueman was brought back and, with the entire ground sensing that the battle was at its height, bowled magnificently. Twice in an over Sobers was beaten outside off stump. Then, edging one that flew, he saw the ball travel straight in and straight out of Close's hands at first slip. Close's brow stayed broodingly low for several overs. Twenty minutes later he was reprieved, as Sobers drove at a full length ball and England won an appeal for a catch by Parks. Sobers, standing his ground, looked unhappy with the decision. West Indian booing emphasised the importance of this dismissal, with Sobers out at 84 for 4. Solomon, the best anchor in this West Indies XI, was now sent in ahead of Worrell; he lasted until tea but not much longer, as Stewart at short-leg took the sharpest of catches off Allen. With the score now 104 for 5, England definitely held their strongest position since the match began, perhaps the strongest position either side had enjoyed.

Worrell's appearance was dignified, almost somnolent. Did he suggest calm? Or, in the twilight of his career, vagueness and uncertainty? Spectators of each persuasion read what they wished. The match, it seemed, hinged on the answer. In the first innings Worrell had been instantly 'done' by Trueman. This time, though he all but edged Allen in his first over, the bone china held up to Trueman's assault. The famous late cut began to function, and the smoothly executed sweep.

All the time, since lunch, Butcher was in occupation at the other end. It began to dawn on the crowd, and perhaps the England team, that they had been watching the wrong man. Against Trueman, especially, Butcher was strong on the leg-side. In all, he was to take five fours off Trueman between square-leg and long-on, and on the off side a single only. Against the off-spinners, using his feet shrewdly, he steadily gathered ones and twos into the mid-wicket area and down to fine-leg. And against Allen, he twice jumped out to clout straight sixes far into the Caribbean crowd. The mood at the Nursery end was once again joyful. 'NNOH!' exalted the chorus when Butcher dug out one that was cutting back or keeping low. Often he played his defensive shots with an almost exaggerated care. The contrast between attack and defence was abrupt, quite different from Worrell's even tenor; and once Butcher dashed far down the pitch, only to be saved from stumping by an edge which travelled through slip for four. Often enough, the captain spoke with Butcher, reminding him of his continuing responsibility, and he even ordered a drink out for him. So, Butcher went to his hundred – made out of 154 – and on even further, in the only big innings of the match.

England, again, had surrendered ground when they were forced to rest Trueman and Shackleton in preparation for the new ball; West Indies had profited from Allen and Titmus bowling in harness for the first time in the match. But this time the new ball held no salvation for England. Six overs with it at the end of the day simply provided a succession of strokes of the purest timing, sending Butcher on to 129, and the West Indies up to 214 for 5. Within the course of the final session, Butcher and Worrell had added 110 in a hundred minutes, and completely overturned England's supremacy. They now claimed the strongest position either side had held in the game.

Come Monday morning, and another huge crowd saw another astonishing reversal. In 25 minutes, the last five wickets had gone to Shackleton and Trueman for only 15 runs. It started on Trueman's third ball of the day to Worrell, when Stewart parried and then caught a blur of a catch at short-leg. It ended, to all intents and purposes, when Butcher sought to make haste amid the falling wickets and was clamorously lbw to Shackleton. Trueman's five wickets in the innings made 11 in the match, for 152 runs. Butcher's 133, though, had not only saved his side from almost certain defeat, it had given them a position from which they were now likely to win. The 234 which England needed was a higher score than anyone had ever made to win a Test at Lord's. In fact, not since 1902 had England made as many to win *any* Test on English soil.

Still, precedent aside, the task was feasible. The pitch was lasting fairly well – not, as expected, favouring the spinners, but continuing to give some encouragement to the fast men. To stem the torrent of Hall and Griffith at the start would be paramount. Lunch was an important summit; this time England had the best part of the morning session to play through. Stewart and Edrich withstood the initial barrage. But by lunch they were both gone, Edrich again caught down the leg side, Stewart unluckily ducking a bouncer only for the ball to ricochet off the top of his bat handle. And by lunch, Dexter also was gone. This time there was almost inevitably an air of anticlimax; he stood as the non-striker for nearly a quarter of an hour before receiving his first ball, was confronted straightaway with spin and soon drove over a ball from Gibbs. Though Cowdrey remained immune to the threat of Gibbs and a bracket of tauntingly close catchers, and Barrington suddenly fired off three fours against Gibbs, the lunchtime position of 47 for 3 was really just as bad as Englishmen had feared, making their chances of defying history almost negligible.

The memory of Dexter lashing Hall and Griffith on Friday seemed but a dream. The two were again as armed assassins. Worse, for England, Hall seemed never to tire. At least, after lunch, Barrington stood up to him. The fact that he did not look to be enjoying it made the merit greater, and the tension. Englishmen in the crowd were now ready to shout for every boundary, as they did when Cowdrey, beginning to spread his wings, placed Gibbs for three fours in an over. The score was scarcely 70, still far from threatening the distant peak of 234; but, in this taut atmosphere, the batsmen's increasing resistance to Hall now caused him to drop the ball short. Worrell supported him with close fieldsmen on the leg and off. Unless the ball was short enough to hook, the batsman had the choice of fending with the bat, letting the ball hit him, or leaving it. The murky background of the pavilion was no help. Barrington had been cracked once on the hand and Hall had bowled seven short balls in succession when the eighth – not terribly short – rose sharply and Cowdrey, instinctively raising his left arm for protection, was struck above the wrist. The sound of the blow suggested, correctly, a broken bone.

Close replaced Cowdrey at the wicket. Barrington the Steadfast, as if sensing the crowd's support, took England's revenge out on Gibbs; from middle-stump, he twice pulled him savagely for six, the first into the crowd, the second high up into the Grand Stand – then swung again, only just over Hall's head at mid-off. Hall came off, after bowling 16 overs at undiminished speed. Griffith, replacing him, searched for the yorker. Barrington jammed them out. Close's defence was as stern, while Barrington went to his 50 in the rapid time of 90 minutes. Two interruptions for bad light brought play finally to a halt at a quarter to five. England were 116 for 3, having lost no wickets since the third at 31. But they had lost Cowdrey, and although they were half way to victory, no one could say what the outcome would be on the last day.

There was more light rain overnight and in the morning but, though it delayed the start of play, it failed to seriously dampen the playing area and it failed to dampen the sense of anticipation. The game resumed at 20 minutes past two. Barrington and Close were the batsmen. Again Hall and Griffith shared the attack. One abiding memory of the match would be of Hall's long walk back and the lithe, bounding stride eating up the ground from the pavilion to the bowling crease; he bowled from the start to the end of play, with unvarying rhythm and speed. At the outset, neither bowler nor batsmen made progress. Barrington batted as if suffering delayed reaction from the previous afternoon's battle. He stayed, jumpily, on the back foot, his strokes late and hasty. His first scoring stroke came after 45 minutes, an involuntary single off his glove. No sooner had he followed this with a happier shot, turning a half-volley through square-leg for four, than he tried to make room to cut and was caught behind. The clock showed a quarter past three and the scoreboard 130 for 4: only 14 runs in almost an hour, and only 13 overs bowled in this time.

Close had scarcely faced Hall the previous afternoon, when Barrington had been the dominant partner. Now all the pressure was on him, the last major batsman and reputedly a good player of fast bowling. There was the pressure also of a career in which he was often thought to have disappointed. His 'character' was on the line. Now he took Hall almost continually; he played within the line of his stumps, keeping his bat out of danger on either side, and when Hall dropped short he let the ball thump him in the ribs. True to his reputation, he seemed almost to relish showing Hall that the ball could be played as happily with the body as with the bat. And perhaps it was in further recognition of his role that he ignored possible short singles to stay at 'Hall's end'. At tea he had played 65 balls, all but 11 overs, of Hall's 14 successive overs.

With him, Parks had found some success on his natural front foot, twice putting Griffith past cover for handsome fours. But when looking positively confident, on 17, Parks was lbw trying to turn to leg a ball from Griffith that kept low. England were 158 for 5, with the match in balance. Titmus was as acquisitive as Parks had been, and he made Close respond to the short singles. But runs were still desperately hard to come by, especially with many deliveries from Hall going un-hittably down the leg side, and by tea England had added only 55 in nearly two hours, while losing two wickets. The five wickets down for 171 were virtually six, with Cowdrey's injury. There remained 63 runs to score in less than 90 minutes – or, more relevantly, in about 20 overs if Hall and Griffith continued to do most of the bowling.

Close, 35 at tea, now slipped the leash. No longer could the fast ball down the leg side be ignored, not when it tempted his favourite shot. Variously it would be described as a hook, a sweep, a pull. He called it the 'lap'. From front or back foot the ball was helped on its way, in the air, down to long leg. A 'West Indian' shot, perhaps, it was much more distinctive amongst English professionals. Now he swung Hall to that boundary; then swung and missed twice in succession; swung again, and prompted a spectacular high-speed pick-up by Butcher on the line. When Griffith bowled, Hall himself, with unlimited energy, swooped likewise to save the boundary. Close swung again at Hall, and the ball, bouncing low, struck his pad. To a raucous appeal, while Close rubbed his thigh at a generous height, the umpire remained unmoved. Yet again Close swung, getting this one to the fine-leg boundary and reaching his 50. Off Gibbs, who had relieved Griffith, he had cut to the boundary, and now 'lapped' four runs more.

England had reached 200. Even counting Cowdrey's wicket as making six down, they were now winning. Hall's walk back had grown weary, even if the velocity of his run-up was still heroically maintained. Titmus had been playing him with formality, until he now turned him upwards into the leg trap for McMorris to cling to the catch at chest height. The next batsman was Trueman; his first ball was on a perfect length, just outside off stump, and Trueman's edge sent all West Indians in the air. In two balls England, 203 for 7, were no longer winning. But they *could* win, if Close stayed in. The new batsman was Allen, number 10.

Close's response, as Hall raced in to start a new over, was to start walking down the wicket to him. It was the most extraordinary of counters, and scarcely necessary; it was, perhaps, less a tactical than a spiritual response. He was, in a sense, running *at* his assailant, and it was too much for Hall, who pulled away in his run-up as if he had been fired at. His expression was anguish and bewilderment; and then he held his back. Worrell came over to comfort him, and Hall went back to his mark apparently restored in limb if not also in mind. Close, inscrutable, advanced again, and again, with his bat in the 'charge' position. Shortening the distance, he was safely protecting his stumps, but he could only swing hazardously as the ball passed on either side.

Griffith came back to continue a fast attack for which Gibbs had provided just five overs' respite. Against Griffith, Close's 'lap' now picked up the ball like a sweep off a slower bowler and it sailed to the corner boundary, almost for six and almost a catch. Swinging and swinging, sometimes missing and sometimes snicking, he now wafted Hall again to long-leg – his fourth four off him to that boundary.

Worrell had been forced to push his field deeper, allowing more singles. With Allen staying scoreless but safe, Close had added all 16 runs since the last wicket, and England, needing 15 runs in 20 minutes, were now winning again . . . Then Close, against Griffith, swung for the last time, getting only a touch off the bottom edge for a catch to Murray. He wheeled away and was off as the shouts echoed. In just under two hours to tea he had stayed firm to score 28 runs, in just over an hour after tea he had made 35, with six fours. He had been pilloried before for his failures and now, in once again playing 'his way', he had all but won a famous victory; and for all the disappointment at his getting out, the now understanding and appreciative Members' Pavilion rose to him.

The West Indies XI, regrouped excitedly at the wicket, now again sensed victory. Only tail-enders stood in their way. Hall and Griffith sought the good length, straight, fast ball. Allen and Shackleton strove first to keep them out, and second, if possible, to snatch singles. Though the crowd held its breath with every ball, it would seem, when the match was over, that for the bowlers the required ball was as beyond them as were the runs for the batsmen. Both sides had blown themselves out. And although Shackleton and Allen made a nominal attempt for eight runs in the last over, and Shackleton was run out, and Cowdrey dramatically came in with plastered arm to watch as Allen safely played the last two balls, the match ended with England 228 for 9: five runs away from a tie and six from victory. Many times though the draw may be viewed as an unsatisfactory outcome, this time, by unanimous consent of both sides and all spectators, it was the proper result to an unforgettable Test match.

N. H.

TWO FOR THE GODS

Australia v England, Sydney, December 1903

On 17 December 1903, the Wright brothers became the first men to achieve a controlled, sustained, powered flight when their flimsy biplane flew for 12 seconds at Kitty Hawk, North Carolina. (Sir George Cayley's British Coachman's Carrier, which flew in 1853, has lately been accepted as a precedent, but the Wright brothers' epic, made known universally in 1906, remains a popular milestone in aviation history.) That 12-second achievement, however, gives way in the hearts of cricket-followers to a seven-hour marathon by a batsman playing in his first Test match, at Sydney, on the other side of the Pacific Ocean. The match, full of incident, ended on the day that Orville Wright became airborne, and immortalised Reginald Erskine Foster, 25, of Malvern, Oxford University, and Worcestershire. His innings of 287 remains unequalled as a maiden-Test offering.

The 1903–04 team in Australia, led by P. F. Warner, was the first to be sent under the MCC flag. It came to the first Test undefeated and with three large victories under its belt, but with England having lost the four preceding series against Australia there was an extra determination to reverse the trend. The side was a strong one, though it lacked the services of the three great amateurs Fry, Jackson, and MacLaren; yet Australia boasted the greatest batsman in the world in Trumper and probably the most effective all-rounder in M. A. Noble.

The sun shone and a firm pitch awaited the players as Noble and Warner tossed. With doubtful weather forecast, the winning of the toss was expected to give a sizable advantage to the side batting first. It became Australia's privilege when Warner lost the toss, but before four overs had been completed England had a strong grip on the game.

Ted Arnold of Worcestershire bowled the second over after

Hirst of Yorkshire had conceded a run each to Duff and Trumper in the opening over, and with his first ball in Test cricket Arnold took the prized wicket of Trumper, who was magnificently caught left-handed by Foster at slip.

With the first ball of his second over Arnold, who could make the ball leave the bat at a brisk pace, had Duff caught behind by Lilley. When Hirst chipped in with Hill's wicket, also taken by the wicket-keeper, Australia floundered at 12 for 3 wickets.

Then came a revival. Noble, who went on to get 133, added 106 with Armstrong (48), and 82 with Hopkins, before the number six was bowled by Hirst with the new ball. It was a gritty fight back, Noble making only ten runs in his first three-quarters of an hour at the crease.

Towards the end of the day the skies darkened, and Noble sent for Bill Howell, the hitter, to come in at number seven. But he holed out to Arnold's bowling, and Gregory came in to make 23 before meeting the same fate as Armstrong – bowled by Bosanquet's googly, the new 'mystery' ball which, though bowled with a leg-break action, turned in from the off. Australia went to bed 259 for 6, and honours could be said to be fairly even once more.

There were storms during the night, and though the morning was clear as play recommenced, one end of the pitch had been visibly affected. The remaining four Australian wickets were taken for only 26 runs, leaving the home side 285 all out; Arnold took 4 for 76, having dismissed Noble through another superb catch by Foster, this time at short-leg.

Warner and Hayward began England's reply, but unhappily for England's captain, in his first Test match, he was caught at the wicket off Laver without scoring. In came Tyldesley, the brilliant little Lancastrian, and masterfully did he bat, timing a wide range of strokes to perfection and seeing Laver and the menacing left-armer Saunders out of the attack. Noble confided later that on that damp pitch he fully expected Saunders to take four wickets before lunch.

Hayward was bowled by off-spinner Howell 10 minutes before lunch, and Foster was to have gone in next; but Warner held him back, sending in Arnold. England were 58 for 2 at the break.

Tyldesley's was the wicket Australia wanted quickly, and Noble himself did the trick, bowling him for 53 with an 'arm ball'. That was the breakthrough. Although the wicket was easing all the time, England were over 200 behind with three men out. Now R. E. Foster entered, recognised by many of the 36,000 present for his stylish 35 in the New South Wales match. He was not entirely comfortable for some time.

Foster and Arnold were to add 44 for the fourth wicket before the fast bowler, who batted an hour and a half for his 27, was caught at fine short-leg off Armstrong. England 117 for 4.

Now came the partnership that was to place England's name on the match, barring mishaps. Foster, surviving those early scrapes, warmed to his task and began stroking the ball in an ominously commanding manner, while Len Braund showed why he was considered a true all-rounder. The afternoon was no longer just warm; it was hot and steamy. And the flies took a close look at the cricketers – to their annoyance. At tea the total had been 135 for 4, yet by the close of the second day's play England were 243, Braund having opened up in the last 20 minutes. Foster was 73 not out, giving no real hint as to what lay ahead, and Braund was 67.

Foster had not been everyone's choice for the tour, though he had several times proved to be a man for an occasion. In his first Gentlemen v Players match he scored 102 and 136, having made 171 in the University match 10 days earlier. His outstanding seasons were 1900 and 1901, but his business as a stockbroker was to keep him from full-time cricket for the years still left to him. He was not only the most gifted of a remarkable brotherhood of seven (all of whom played for Worcestershire – sometimes known as 'Fostershire'!) but on his form in this Sydney Test match he was justly referred to as 'the English Trumper'. There could be no higher praise.

After a Sunday's rest, Foster and Braund continued their partnership on what turned out to be, in Warner's proud words, 'a record-extinguishing day'. England's highest Test total (576 v Australia, at The Oval, 1899) was beaten; the fifth-wicket record (162 by MacLaren and Peel, Melbourne, 1894–95) was beaten; the last-wicket record was broken (and still stands to the credit of Foster and Rhodes in England–Australia Tests – 130); and, most memorably, Foster's score of 287 was by far the highest innings played in a Test. It was to remain so until the 1929–30 series in West Indies, when Andrew Sandham made 325 for England. Don Bradman's 334 a few months later eclipsed Foster's score as an England–Australia record.

So much for the figures and the landmarks. How did R. E. 'Tip' Foster make those runs? His captain, 'Plum' Warner, summed it up thus: 'His batting on the Monday was, I think, the best I have ever seen; his off-driving and cutting have never been equalled – of that I feel sure – while there was a Lyons-like power about his straight driving. On the on side, too, he was wonderfully good, frequently forcing the ball away in a masterly manner. His style was, as it always is, beautifully easy, and he made good use of his exceptional quickness of foot, frequently moving a yard out of his ground to play the ball.'

Australia's Frank Iredale could not recall such a superb innings that had begun so badly. For the first two hours Foster batted on the Saturday he seemed likely to get out at any time. He was hesitant in his strokeplay, over-reached himself in playing forward, and became agitated at the persistency of flies. 'To show to what a high pitch of brilliancy he rose', wrote Iredale, 'I may say he carried the people with him. No greater proof of greatness is there than this.'

Foster obtained his century with a beautiful, wristy cut off Laver, and Braund, his partner, went from 94 to 102 with two dazzling off-drives in the next over. Then Howell yorked him. The record stand of 192 took England to 309 for 5 – 24 ahead. Australia then climbed back into the reckoning by taking three wickets for 23: Hirst was bowled by Howell, and Noble had Bosanquet and Lilley caught. In came Albert Relf of Sussex, a good man to be in at number 10. He stayed with Foster while 115 were added, making only 31 himself, but seeing his partner take the Australian bowling and shake it till it rattled. Foster passed Charles Bannerman's 165, then Ranjitsinhji's 175, then Syd Gregory's 201 (off Gregory's own bowling!), before Relf fell to Saunders on the stroke of tea, when England were 447 for 9, Foster 203. One more wicket and Australia's torture would be ended.

In fact, that final wicket took them 66 minutes to get. Wilfred Rhodes, Yorkshire's young left-arm slow bowler, who was to open England's innings before his glorious career ended, was no easy victim for the home side's impatient bowlers. Nor did he simply hold an end up while Foster stormed along. Of the 130 runs added, 40 were Rhodes's – and he was left 'not out'!

Foster left W. L. Murdoch's Test record of 211 behind with a hook to the boundary off Armstrong, and there seemed no way the Australians could hope to dismiss him. The 500 came, to generous applause, and the pair took 16 off an over by the Penrith beekeeper, Howell. Foster hit 15 off an over from medium-pacer Laver. Soon England's previous record of 576 was passed, and Foster's triple-century was in sight. Only 13 such scores had been registered in the history of first-class cricket. But with the laxity that comes with fatigue and anticlimax, Foster spooned the left-arm medium-pacer Saunders to Noble at mid-off. His 287 had lasted just over seven hours, and included 37 fours – six of them successive scoring strokes taking him from 126 to 150. Even Len Hutton in his 364 in 1938 hit only 35 boundaries. As for number 11, Rhodes, he remembered his part proudly until his dying day (in 1973).

Facing arrears of 292, Australia were a stubborn 108 for 2 by lunch on the following day, having lost the night-watchmen openers Gregory and Kelly. Hill and Duff built the total to 191, when Duff (84) was caught at short-leg off Rhodes, and it was clear that on a near-perfect wicket the Australians would have to be prised out. Their number five batsman was Victor Trumper. With him out, England would have a crystal-clear sight of victory.

But not content with one stupendous innings in this Test match, whoever was responsible decreed that Trumper would play perhaps the most exquisite of his many heavenly innings. In his first 20 minutes at the crease, until tea was taken, he made a careful seven, and his side was 207 for 3 – still 85 behind. He was cautious for a time after the interval, then, while Clem Hill ran his runs fast and shut an end up, Trumper began to flow. Rhodes kept him watchful, but off Relf he took runs as if it were a picnic match. Braund came on, but his first over had crazy results: Trumper cut the first ball sweetly for four, and treated the next the same; the third went for four byes, and the fourth was struck through extra cover for four more; Trumper played the fifth ball back down the pitch; then came the last ball of the over: Trumper again forced past mid-off, and the batsmen ran hard – one, two, three – then an attempt at a fourth. But Hirst returned the ball from the outfield to Braund, who had a shy at the stumps. It missed, and the batsmen attempted a fifth run from the overthrow – though Hill had run well past the wicket in racing home for the fourth. Relf gathered the ball and threw to wicket-keeper Lilley, and as the bails flew and the appeal went up, umpire Bob Crockett raised his finger.

Hill, a fiery fellow, said nothing, but his demeanour as he left the field showed that he felt he had been safe. The crowd took up the cause, and soon there were hisses, groans, loud catcalls, and cries of 'Crock! Crock! Crock!' 'How much did you pay Crockett, Warner?' and 'Have you got your coffin ready, Crockett?' echoed over the field, prompting Warner to walk to the pavilion, where even some members had loudly been having their say. He was getting nowhere, so he walked back to the wicket with Noble, the next man in, and there they waited for a few minutes, hoping for the demonstrations to subside. Eventually play was resumed, but the incident was not forgotten. Shouts continued to ring out from those who were not completely enchanted by Trumper's strokeplay – these were not true cricket-lovers. Of the 81 added for the fifth wicket, Noble made only 22 before being stumped off Bosanquet. Trumper cut, drove, glanced, played with effortless power from a position right back on his stumps, made all bowlers except Rhodes look like schoolboys. He was 119 not out by the end of the afternoon, Armstrong 14, Australia 367 for 5 – ahead by 75. In the hundred minutes since tea Trumper had made 112 runs, 64 of them in the final 40 minutes. Foster must have eyed him with mixed feelings as Trumper must have eyed Foster for a day and a half.

Overnight rain bound the pitch a little, and helped the daisies which were springing up in the outfield; but with over 1200 runs having already been made on it the pitch was not going to remain a batsman's paradise for much longer. Every minute that Trumper and his partners stayed in occupation, England's task would be less appetising. Trumper did stay, but fortunately for England none of his all-too-human partners did. Rhodes had Armstrong caught at slip, and Hirst lured Hopkins into a catch to cover point. Laver was taken at slip off the persevering Rhodes, and Howell was caught behind off Arnold, and when Jack Saunders was slow to respond to a strike-stealing call from Trumper he was run out, leaving his senior 185 not out, made in only 230 minutes, with 25 fours. He had reached 50 in an hour, hit 18 off Braund's next over, and raced to his century in 94 minutes, still the third-fastest century in England–Australia Tests.

Thanks to Victor Trumper, Sydney's 26-year-old, smooth-faced cricketing god, England had a task before them if they were to win a match that had seemed safe 24 hours before. They almost didn't make it. Four wickets, including R. E. Foster's, went fairly cheaply, and if Hirst had been caught by the usually reliable Laver at short-leg off Howell before he had scored (he would have 'bagged a pair') England would have been lurching at 83 for 5. Laver put it down, and Hirst (60 not out) and Tom Hayward (91) put on 99 before the latter was stumped on the sixth morning. It was a scholarly, chanceless, four-hour innings, but unluckily for Hayward it came in the same match as Foster's and Trumper's.

George Hirst, broadshouldered and defiant, hit the winning runs, and England were home by five wickets. They won the second Test as well, lost the third, won the fourth, also at Sydney, and with it the Ashes, and lost the fifth. It was an action-packed series. Yet one wonders how much the overall success owed this opening contest.

Neither of the two batting heroes, Foster and Trumper, was to live to 40; they died almost within a year of each other in 1914–15. Trumper's death shook Australia, and the route taken by his funeral cortège was lined by row upon row of people.

Foster had faded from the public eye some years before his passing, in London on 13 May 1914, from diabetes. Insulin had yet to be discovered. He had played only three more times for England, captaining the side against South Africa in the 1907 series, thus becoming the only man to have led England at cricket and association football (he was a brilliant inside-forward for Corinthians and gained six caps for England at the turn of the century).

Fortunate were those who saw not only Trumper's dazzling innings at Sydney in December 1903 but Foster's double-century – and, a detail which should never be forgotten, Foster's magnificent catch which sent Trumper back for only a single in the first innings. When he snared that lightning snick from Trumper's bat, flying faster than the Wright brothers' machine at Kitty Hawk, he might well have been capturing the match for England.

A.T.

THE LAST HALF HOUR

England v Australia, The Oval, April 1968

Since the War, England had won precious few Tests against Australia at home. The milestones were The Oval in 1953; Headingley and Old Trafford in Laker's series of 1956; and Headingley again in 1961. Out of 29 Tests, only four victories. In this summer of 1968 a well-rounded England side, after losing the first Test at Manchester, had been on top pretty well throughout the next three, without gaining the result. At Lord's and Edgbaston rain had denied them almost certain victories. So, by the fourth and final Test at The Oval they could, at best, only level the series, with Australia retaining the Ashes. Still, the victory was keenly sought, and Australia were as determined to prevent it.

From the time that England won the toss and batted, on a gorgeous high summer day, Australia were always to be on the back foot to a greater or lesser extent, and England always pressing, with greater or lesser prospects, to open up the road to victory. The first day belonged to Edrich, less reliant than usual on pushes and nudges, letting the bat swing into firm drives and square cuts. His hundred was his sixth for England and his fourth against Australia, emphasising that he is at his best when it really matters. On the second day, D'Oliveira followed him past 150 in an innings which contained several chances but was, none the less, typically calm yet emphatic. England made 494.

Just as the England innings had been essentially Edrich's, so Australia's belonged to their opening batsman Lawry. More so than any other batsman, he seemed to clearly indicate his intention to stay at the crease for a long time. As always, his bat was close to his front foot, the blade angled down behind that foot, the peaked cap and the hawk-like nose thrusting down over the shot; his judgment of length was sure, his self-discipline and concentration as constant as the minutes which ticked through the entire day. Not so, some of his colleagues'. At the end of the day Australia were 264 for 7, just 34 away from saving the follow-on, and with Lawry still in occupation, after seven and a quarter hours for 135, England seemed to have too little time left to force victory.

On the Monday morning Lawry was out without addition. But the fact that the last four Australian wickets added 136, the last two 55 (lasting nearly two hours), did nothing to encourage prospects of an England victory. Now, as England began their second innings, there remained only 10 hours in the match. England's innings was very short but satisfactorily brisk. No one made above 35, but in just three hours they totalled 181. Some critics felt that for all the urgency of England's second innings, Cowdrey had been too conservative in continuing so far towards the end of the day. An earlier declaration, giving Australia an hour's batting before the close and the prospect of scoring in all around 320 at 45 an hour, might well have kept them interested the next day – and brought wickets. As it was, they needed 352 at 54 an hour, scarcely feasible in a Test.

Such arguments were soon forgotten. Snow's first over was meticulously played by Inverarity. Then Lawry faced Brown and, after playing the first ball most securely through mid-off for four, played forward to the next. Again the pad and bat were in the closest proximity, but this time the ball spooned slightly and Milburn at close short-leg dived like a large fish to scoop the ball up in his right hand. Lawry's dismissal had probably increased England's chances of winning the match, diminished Australia's of saving it, by 25 per cent. Redpath, who with Lawry had made almost two-thirds of Australia's first innings runs, batted with authority until the last over of the day. To Underwood's third ball he elected to play with the pad a quicker ball close to leg stump, which straightened. With the shout and the umpire's finger, Australia were 13 for 2, and England in this instant could see the open road to victory.

Next morning, Underwood's unfinished over proved enlightening. The new batsman, Ian Chappell, straightaway got a ball that spun sharply and from the edge of the bat fell just short of Cowdrey at slip. Perhaps it was this fright, or perhaps just his customary technique, which soon caused Chappell to go back to Underwood's quicker ball, to be palpably lbw. Walters stayed for half an hour for one run, playing the ball from the pitch, making late and hurried adjustments, before Underwood produced a killer ball which stood up and twisted from leg to off stump, and Walters did well, technically, to get an edge to it. Knott took the sharp catch excellently up around his right shoulder. Australia were 29 for 4, with the match rapidly winding up.

Inverarity was holding fast, though. His had not been the most fruitful of tours, and his Test opportunities were few. His stroke play and his demeanour were modest, though perhaps it was his glasses which made him look un-Australian. Now he played with the straightest of bats and a calm, pragmatic policy. First and foremost, he guarded the line of his stumps. His bat was well sheltered. If the ball turned and lifted – as one tended to do every over or so from Underwood – then that was all right. Inverarity's bat did not follow it; the ball simply passed by, making it almost impossible to say that he had been beaten. With him was Sheahan. They were the last *bona fide* batsmen, Australia's only hope for a long, match-saving partnership. But long-term survival was asking a lot, when England could afford to keep a close ring of fieldsmen around the bat. For Underwood, there were seven and sometimes eight men within four yards; Illingworth had three on the leg side plus slip and gully. Perhaps some of the close men were too close. Once Dexter at silly point, moving forward, got a technical chance off bat and pad, making hand contact with a ball that must have been only a blur. It was Inverarity's only chance in the two and a half hours of the morning session. Sheahan was less certain in defence, but played some firm strokes to break up the field. It was in attempting another that he fell; rather unluckily for him, he pulled Illingworth skimmingly within reach of Snow at mid-wicket, and the only man anywhere in that territory made a good catch low down on the move.

Wicket-keeper Jarman joined Inverarity. He soon gave a difficult low chance which Knott could not hold, and defended uncertainly; but he did give himself some confidence by hitting well to leg when Underwood strayed. As lunch approached the sky grew sultry over the gasometers. At first it looked like heat haze, and the few spots which caused them to go into lunch just a minute early did not seem ominous. But the sky then grew dark, and shortly the rain was pelting down with tropical vigour. In half an hour the ground was practically under water. Through the rain, the still scoreboard showed Australia 86 for 5.

Though the cloud-burst had done its work and been followed by clearer skies, the outfield was like a swamp. Many spectators went home. Journalists, players, and others concerned themselves with travel arrangements. But, as the sky now promised to remain clear and sunny, and the pitch covers were drawn back to reveal a surface moistened by seepage but certainly not unplayable, there emerged at least the possibility of mopping up the outfield. There were acres of it, of course – seven and a half, to be precise – and a ground staff of only four. Groundsman Ted Warn went among the crowd and asked for assistants. He soon had all he needed – about 50 – taking off their shoes and rolling up trousers to step forward on to the soggy field. The main means of attack was the pitchfork, puncturing below the top surface to try to get the water to seep deeper. Other efforts to *lift* water were made with blankets and foam rubber. At last, towards four o'clock, the umpires decided that play might resume at a quarter to five, if there was no further rain. There was none, and so Inverarity and Jarman came out to play for six o'clock. England had an hour and a quarter to take five wickets. Would the pitch take turn?

Immediately it was obvious that the wicket was nearly sodden, without any sun now to invigorate it, and the ball also was damp. Inverarity's bat was immediately as straight as it had been in the morning; Jarman's almost as straight, though a little anxious. Anxiety was caused more than anything by the ring of fieldsmen around the bat – all 10, excluding the bowler, standing shoulder to shoulder. This at least was the field for Underwood. Illingworth had just one man out, to try to save the single and keep Jarman at strike. Now and then one of these close catchers dived forward to try to snatch the ball as it went to ground from a defensive bat, but there were mainly futile gestures creating spurious impressions of danger. Underwood bowled from one end. At the other, three bowlers alternated in the course of five overs. No breakthrough had been made after 35 minutes. It was 20 past five and Cowdrey might well have been concluding that if Australia were still only five wickets down at half-past five, the extra half hour would not be worth claiming. D'Oliveira came on at Underwood's end, the fifth bowler and the sixth change in 40 minutes. Then Illingworth bowled an over in which Inverarity survived a chance that Dexter dived and grabbed for, and the next ball whipped past the shoulder of his bat. The pitch was coming to life.

D'Oliveira bowled again, to Jarman: a smooth floater, Jarman's bat stayed limp, almost leaving the ball, and the ball clipped the top of the off stump. The ended partnership had been worth almost 45 runs, and much more in time. The real tail were now coming in, cold, and now that D'Oliveira had done his job Underwood took over from him. Underwood's second ball stopped, causing Mallett to lift his defensive shot into the hands of Brown at short-leg. To the last ball of this same over McKenzie also pushed forward, and this time Brown took an extremely agile catch, diving and rolling to emerge with the ball held out dramatically in his left hand.

England now needed only two more wickets, in 25 minutes. Gleeson, who had walked in at a sporting pace, now played with shrewd and aggravating use of the pad, and also occasionally pushed one through the close field to get away from the bowling. Inverarity did not look like getting out. Occasionally hitting well to leg, he reached his 50. The partnership had taken the time almost up to 10 minutes to six. Underwood, frustrated, went to change to over the wicket. Cowdrey waved him back to continue around. With his next ball he deceived Gleeson with his line and pace and knocked back the off stump. Twelve minutes remained when the wicket fell, 10 as last man Connolly took guard. There was one ball left in Underwood's over, and Connolly survived it.

Illingworth bowled from the other end to Inverarity, who played three balls and then took a single off the fourth. Connolly played the last two safely.

With six minutes remaining – offering two, at the most three, overs – and Inverarity to face Underwood, England's chances seemed to have receded. But still the pressure was immense, the entire England side encircling the batsman, the crowd quite silent, and Underwood with immaculate length making the batsmen play every ball. *Start* to play it, at any rate, for Inverarity's judgment was permitting him to alter his decision late in the shot. Always in his mind was the alternative of dropping the bat and thrusting the pad out. He had gone in first and stayed while better batsmen had failed, he had been batting for four hours and 10 minutes, and in another five minutes he would have saved his country and made himself famous. It was too much.

As Underwood bowled over the wicket, a ball fairly well up on middle and off stump, Inverarity started to play it and then lifted his bat and jabbed out the pad. It was a compulsive movement, almost an aberration. He must have known, even as he did it, that the ball was in line to come on with the arm instead of turning away; certainly he knew as the shout went up from the 11 Englishmen who surrounded him. The shout was not an appeal but an acclamation – and Inverarity, who had turned his back, did not look at the umpire. Inverarity was out for 56, Australia were all out for 125, Underwood had taken seven wickets for 50 in 31½ overs, and England had at last snatched an elusive victory against Australia.

N. H.

NAPPER'S PRIVATE WARS

Australia v England, Sydney, December 1932
South Africa v Australia, Johannesburg,
December 1935
England v Australia, Nottingham, July 1938

He looked quite the part in his sports shop in George Street, Sydney, below the Cricketers Club of New South Wales. Medium height, bald (he had been since early manhood), comfortably built, with a round, genial face. Hardly the classic hero to look at. Yet Stanley Joseph McCabe played not just one, or two, but *three* Test innings of such power and daring that any of the great batsmen in cricket history would have been proud to call just one his own. Indeed, in the last, the fury of his strokeplay in adversity prompted Don Bradman himself to call to his card-playing colleagues, 'Come and look at this. You may never see its like again'.

Strength of character ran in the family, for McCabe's grandmother, an outstanding pioneer bushwoman, had taken her three children from Melbourne through hundreds of miles in a buggy to the New South Wales country town of Grenfell, across scrubland and hill, fording the mighty River Murray, and surviving the night attention of three armed bushrangers. Catherine died in 1928, aged 94, the grandmother of 37 children.

Young Stan was chosen to tour England in 1930 before he had made a century and before his twentieth birthday. He played in all five Tests and impressed, and was kept in the side for the home series against West Indies and South Africa. Then, in 1932-33, came Douglas Jardine's Englishmen with their threat of bodyline bowling – fast deliveries in the direction of the batsman, with a cordon of fieldsmen close in to catch the ball as it was parried from the throat or chest. For the hook shot men were placed on the boundary. Leading the assault were Notts fast bowlers Harold Larwood, right-arm, very fast, and deadly accurate, and Bill Voce, large, left-arm, able to swing the new ball in at what sometimes amounted to an unavoidable angle. The principal victim was intended to be Don Bradman, who had made scores of 131, 254, 334, and 232 during the 1930 series, his first in England. Bodyline bowling at least achieved this aim, since Bradman was held to an average of 56.57, well under half his figure in England. But the bitter rancour and disgust which it generated were to last for many, many years.

There were several instances of bravery in the face of this lethal attack. Woodfull, Fingleton, and Vic Richardson all took a battering and yet held on grittily to raise a decent score. But the one truly outstanding innings came in the opening Test match, at Sydney, during the first week of December 1932.

Australia took first use of the wicket, and were 82 for 3 when the 22-year-old country boy went in, saying to his father as he left to get his pads on, 'If I get hit out there you'd better keep Mum from jumping the fence!' He was grimly serious.

Almost immediately the stylish Kippax fell lbw to Larwood, and Australia were struggling at 87 for 4. Vic Richardson, later to be the proud grandfather of the Chappell brothers, joined McCabe.

They added 129, the majority coming from McCabe's flashing bat. He hit hard and often, riding his luck. His hooks were thrilling in their daring and savagery, and he cut viciously. It was like watching a young lion-tamer subduing a rampaging, clawing cageload with only a leather whip and a plywood stool. It was an inglorious season in so many ways, with batsmen dodging and ducking and attempting the weirdest of strokes against this meanest of bowling.

The fiercest eruption – from crowd and Australia's patient and gentlemanly captain, Woodfull – was to come later in the series, at Adelaide, but here at Sydney the sense of outrage was sharp. Australia's only riposte for the time being was McCabe's gallant batsmanship. His luck continued to hold – as it needed to. In just over four hours McCabe made 187 not out, including 60 of the last 70 runs, with 25 boundaries. Australia's total reached an unexpected 360, only once to be exceeded in the entire series; but England piled up 524 (Sutcliffe 194, Hammond 112, Pataudi 102) and dismissed Australia a second time for only 164 (Larwood 5 for 28; McCabe second-top score with 32). This left Jardine's men with one run to make. They went one-up, by 10 wickets, early on the fourth morning. Australia levelled the series at Melbourne, when Bradman made the only other century for Australia that season, and Bill

O'Reilly took five wickets in each innings. But from then onwards it was a runaway for England, who won the remaining three Tests. Legislation against this form of intimidatory bowling followed, but the wounds were slow to heal.

McCabe's glorious innings at Sydney continued for years to evoke paeans of praise. Jack Fingleton described it as 'the greatest I have seen'. Don Bradman wrote, 'I doubt if any other player has more completely subdued a fiery and resolute attack'. A. G. Moyes recalled how 'McCabe risked bodily harm, flicking the fast-rising ball off his eyebrows as one brushes aside the flies with a switch; he beat back the enemy and then drove him in disorder'.

The final stages of the innings were by far the most frenzied. Tim Wall, last man in for Australia, made only four runs in a stand of 55 while McCabe protected him from the bowling, and hooked and pulled with a certainty that disguised the real peril that threatened each time he took on the flying ball. The crowd of 50,000 cheered themselves hoarse, and otherwise staid gentlemen in the members' enclosure got to their feet, clapped till their hands stung, and cried out with joy as the extraordinary innings closed with McCabe unbeaten. He had been dropped only twice – and then late in the innings – in the gully off Voce when 159 and at slip off Larwood when 170. Many a skied hit fell safely. That was to be expected in four hours, and that was where the luck came in, as McCabe was the first to acknowledge. Jardine, for his part, regretted later that he had not placed his field more thoughtfully. Some fieldsmen were in position for mis-hits. Had they been placed for the perfect hook they might have ended the onslaught – albeit at the cost of a bruised or broken finger!

That 187 not out put McCabe among cricket's immortals, and though he continued to show what skills were in him – a double-century for New South Wales against Queensland, when Bradman was not unhappy to be dismissed for nought by a truly fearsome aboriginal fast bowler, Eddie Gilbert, on a poor wicket, was cited as yet another knock which probably no other man on earth could have played – yet it was too much to expect that 'Napper' could perform such a near-miracle again. But he did.

He was nicknamed 'Napper' after wandering off while the Australian touring cricketers were being shown around the Palace of Versailles. When he reappeared through the doorway of Napoleon's bedroom, a smallish, dignified figure with a high forehead, a team-mate quipped that it must be the Little Corporal himself. Thenceforth he was 'Napper'.

It was far from Paris and from Grenfell, the bush town of his birth, that McCabe again burned his name into the annals of heroic hitting. The place was Johannesburg, at the old Wanderers ground, where the main railway station now stands; the date: 28 December 1935.

Australia had won the first Test comfortably, McCabe and Chipperfield scoring hundreds. Indeed, they were to win the last three Tests of the series each by an innings and to go through the tour unbeaten. But in this second Test match, after leading South Africa 250 to 157 on the first innings, they could do nothing to stop Dudley Nourse, who batted for five hours for a record 231 ending when he was caught off McCabe's fast-medium bowling. Eventually Australia were set 399 for victory in little more than a day. That evening, with Bill Brown out for six, Australia were 85, Fingleton in with McCabe, who was 59 already, having reached his half-century in only 42 minutes.

On a treacherous last-day wicket on which the ball sometimes kicked, sometimes shot, often turned almost impossibly sharply, McCabe took the bowlers on and toyed with them. His partner later described his innings as 'miraculous'. Against the pace of Crisp and Langton and the curling slow bowling of Mitchell, he drove and swept, cut and hooked his way to a century in 91 minutes, and 150 in 145 minutes. With Fingleton (40) holding the other end fast, 177 runs were added for the second wicket. With the light fading ominously and the pitch obviously deteriorating fast, it was an absurd expectation – but Australia had the Springboks on the retreat.

Len Darling replaced Fingleton, and McCabe's graceful punishment went on unabated. Louis Duffus summed it up in a paragraph in *The Cricketer*: 'His innings inevitably provided a lesson in calm judgment, unerring placing and powerful strokeplay, executed with a touch of genius. He scored boundaries with such accurate timing and effortless ease that his cricket sometimes appeared cold, yet beneath his undemonstrativeness was a joyous exuberance. He was a striking example of the Australians' adeptness in deciding upon the punishable ball and their ability in reaping the maximum benefit from it.'

After lunch the sky blackened and vivid flicks of lightning cut the backdrop. The final irony was pending. McCabe could still pick out the ball clearly enough from the bowler's hand, but the fieldsmen began to experience difficulty in seeing it from the bat! He and his partner were missed in the slips, and eventually, though it was plain that the approaching thunderstorm would have the last word, and soon South Africa's captain, Herbie Wade, appealed against the light!

They came off, with Australia, 274 for 2, needing just 125 runs in three hours, McCabe 189 not out. Another hour could have brought one of the most sensational victories in Test history. Instead, the rain bucketed down, and 'Napper' unbuckled his pads.

And so to 1938, and his third tour of England. By now he was 28, and acknowledged as one of the finest batsmen of them all, even though he was anything but a seeker of centuries for their own sake. He was an 'occasion' man, most dangerous when things were difficult.

They have seldom been more difficult for Australia than during the first Test of the series, at Trent Bridge, Nottingham, in July. England had amassed 658 for 8 declared, their highest ever against Australia (though to be eclipsed the following month by their 903 for 7 at The Oval). The openers, Barnett and Hutton, made centuries, as did Compton, and Lancashire left-hander Eddie Paynter made 216 not out. Four of Australia's five bowlers conceded over a hundred runs.

Tired by almost nine hours in the field, Australia lost six batsmen before reaching 200. The prized wicket of Bradman was captured for 51, and Brown, 48, had been the only other batsman to make double-figures – except for McCabe. 'Napper' was at it again, attacking, refusing to be controlled. England, under new captain Wally Hammond, had a strong and varied group of bowlers headed by tall fast man Ken Farnes, and with the rapid leg-spin and googly bowling of Doug Wright and the immaculate left-arm spin of Hedley Verity in support (though Verity was held back in this innings, bowling only 7.3 overs).

In bare figures, Stan McCabe scored 232 out of 300 made while he was at the crease. It lasted less than four hours and contained 34 fours and a six; coming in at number four, he soon ran out of senior partners, and until last man Fleetwood-Smith came in his largest partnership had been 69 for the seventh wicket with Ben Barnett, the wicket-keeper, whose 22 was the fourth of four double-figure innings. So many times did McCabe outmanoeuvre the England captain in manipulating the strike, shielding his partners. So many times did he strike the ball cleanly through a gap in the field, leaving the fieldsman to trot after it and return it to the vexed bowler.

He thrillingly hooked Farnes for six, and took 44 runs off three overs from Wright. After reaching his hundred in two hours 20 minutes, he accelerated further! Hammond tried to block him and even delayed taking the new ball. McCabe raced to his double-century in 223 minutes, the second-fastest in Tests after Bradman's 214-minute blitz at Leeds in 1930.

Again, with the McCabe trumpet sounding such a masterful fanfare, it was when the final accompaniment came that the tempo reached its climax. In a mere 28 minutes, 77 runs were battered – of which last man Fleetwood-Smith made but five! In the last 10 overs of the innings McCabe stole the strike in eight; of his 34 boundaries, 16 were struck in that period. It had to end, they had all been saying for a long time. And eventually it did: McCabe cracked a ball from Verity skywards to cover, and to England's relief Compton held it safely. The only other semblance of a chance had been a hook towards Bill Edrich which that fieldsman had made a game effort to hold.

Australia incredibly had reached 411, which was insufficient to avoid the follow-on. But England's moral ascendancy established by their monstrous innings and early breakthrough had been reduced. It was now left to Australia to survive just over eight hours, a task they achieved mainly through Brown and Bradman centuries and an obstinate 40 from Fingleton, who laid down his bat and gloves at one point when the Trent Bridge crowd's barracking at his slow batting became too much. McCabe made 39, caught off Verity, who took 3 for 102 off 67 overs.

So the match was saved, and Australia's victory at Leeds was to secure the Ashes for them as current holders. England's crushing win at The Oval in the final Test did no more than level the series – and create feelings of uneasiness between the two countries. To say nothing of antipathy towards Test matches without time limit!

Stan McCabe played no more Test cricket after 1938. He had always been troubled by flat arches, and his foot ailment together with the loss of years to the war were to mean the end of a splendid international career when he was no more than 28 years old. He had produced something utterly special at Sydney, at Johannesburg, and at Nottingham, something that was to stand out against all the surrounding deeds of high-scoring batsmen from all nations. 'He had come in', wrote Denzil Batchelor after the Trent Bridge innings, 'at a moment in history when it seemed certain that the sun was about to set on a long period of Australian ascendancy. McCabe, by his own efforts, had stopped the sun, and saved the Australian empire.'

Not one of the three matches was won by Australia, though that at Johannesburg was made safe and threatened to be turned into an astonishing victory, and that at Nottingham was unquestionably saved (and probably the series with it). As for the first, at Sydney, against the devilish heat of bodyline, his gallantry assumed an added piquancy as his side eventually went under. There was a resemblance, however faint, with a Victoria Cross won posthumously.

He died after a fall from a cliff at the end of his garden in Mosman, Sydney, on 25 August 1968, aged 58, emaciated by cancer. There was a Test match between England and Australia in progress at The Oval when news came through, and the flags were immediately lowered to half-mast. It so happened that the highest score of his career, 240 for the Australians against Surrey in 1934, was made at that ground.

Among the tributes was one from former opponent Len Hutton, who, describing him as 'a most likeable fellow', wrote: 'He had qualities that even Bradman hadn't got.'

There could be no higher praise for a batsman.

A. T.

INDIAN SUMMER

England v India, The Oval, August 1971

In two short Test series in 1971, against Pakistan and India, England were not a particularly fine side; but they were hard to beat. They had not lost a Test match under Ray Illingworth's experienced and professional captaincy (excepting games against the Rest of the World) and in all they had played 26 Tests without defeat – an unparalleled achievement – when they met India at The Oval.

This was the last of three Tests and, as the previous two had been drawn, the series was also at stake. The drawn matches had favoured England, though there was a continuing problem with the middle of the batting, of which there was very little even in name, in between three opening batsmen and the all-rounders. In the first Test at Lord's England were 71 for 5 before Illingworth and wicket-keeper Knott led them to 304; and at Manchester they were 116 for 5 before the same two rescuers, and Peter Lever, took them up to the dizzy heights of 386. If a pure bowler like Lever could make 88 not out it suggested that England's troubles could be regarded more with amusement than anxiety.

So, India continued to be regarded an 'interesting' side: adequate, often solid batting, supported by a charming array of good slow bowlers. There were two almost equal off-spinners, Venkataraghavan and Prasanna; Bishan Bedi, the left-armer with the turban, the slow flight, immaculate control, and inscrutable calm; and Bhagwat Chandrasekhar, perhaps the most fascinating of the four and certainly the most puzzling. Most difficult to categorise, Chandra bowled with a bent wrist but produced more googlies and top-spinners than he did leg-breaks. Some batsmen said he had to be played 'as an off-spinner'. Fairly tall, and slim, he bowled with his sleeves buttoned down, evidently to cover a right arm wasted by polio.

That long thin shirt sleeve circling high over the top might almost have been a piece of white string with the ball tied at its end. Perhaps Chandra's arm was not so much of a handicap after all; with variations in speed, and a disconcerting degree of bounce, the sling-shot arm was extremely effective.

India's bowlers again offered a fascinating challenge when England batted on the first day at The Oval. They removed that uncertain middle order within minutes when Fletcher was out for one and D'Oliveira for two, and England's first five wickets had fallen for 143. Yet again recovery was led by Knott, with a typically confident and impudent innings of 90 scored in under two hours; and with Richard Hutton encouraging him with an innings of 81, England finished the day in a mood of plunder, all out for 355.

The second day was lost to rain. On the Saturday India's middle order batted most dutifully after losing two wickets for 21, including that of the excellent Gavaskar. Wadekar and Sardesai added 93 and, after Illingworth broke in with three wickets in 23 balls, Solkar and Engineer provided another 97. But when both of these were out just before the close, India at 234 for 7 looked well short of challenging England's 355. Indeed, their effort had to be measured in terms of saving the match, though they could take comfort in the fact that, as one of the newspapers pointed out, three-fifths of the match had gone, and the first two innings had not yet been completed. But Monday was to be another day.

The pitch was slower still on Monday morning. India's not-out batsmen, Venkat and Abid Ali, were able to settle in against the few overs bowled by Snow and Price and then continue their steady progress when Illingworth returned to the bowling crease. They took 13 runs from one over of the off-spinner, which took India past 270. From that point onwards the spinners tightened their grip, and there were only three more scoring strokes in the last nine and a half overs of the innings, as India closed at 284. That partnership of 58 had kept India within sight of England. Within *firing* distance? That would be seen when their spinners went to work again. For England, Underwood had scarcely been able to straighten the ball; Illingworth, with carefully controlled flight, had done much better, thoroughly earning his excellent figures of 5 for 70 off $34\frac{1}{2}$ overs, though he too had found the pitch slow.

Wadekar was quick to try his spinners, giving Abid Ali and Solkar no more than three overs each before turning to Venkat and Chandra. From an arguably defensive position, it was a bold move – especially as in the first innings Jameson had greeted the slow stuff by twice hitting the ball straight into the pavilion. This day he had time only to straight drive Venkat to that same pavilion fence before India were granted good luck from which was to stem genuine success. With the score on an untroubled 23 in the ninth over, Luckhurst drove at Chandra and the ball diverted from the bowler's hand on to the stumps, to dismiss Jameson in the way which is always pure misfortune. Scarcely credible was the fact that Jameson, in each case the innocent party, had been run-out three times in his four Test innings.

This brought in Edrich, an opening batsman who now had to face the spinners straight off. His fifth ball, from Chandra, bowled him off stump. It was a startling dismissal: it may have been a googly, it may have been the top-spinner, but above all Edrich was *yorked* – yorked as conclusively as if by a fast bowler. Fletcher unhappily had to come to the wicket with only a minute remaining to lunch. First ball he pushed forward to what was, in effect, a bouncing off-break and Solkar from short-leg dived forward and made the catch rolling on his back. England were 24 for 3.

It was not just for the possible hat trick that Wadekar pushed men around the bat first ball after lunch. Sensing that England were sliding fast, he determined to keep the pressure at maximum, to let loose Chandra at one end with full attacking support, and to ask Venkat to keep it tight at the other. On the hat trick ball D'Oliveira was saved by his pads. The next ball he jabbed hard to slip, where Sardesai could not hold the very difficult chance – one which damaged his hand – and the ball went for three. Two overs later D'Oliveira had another escape when Solkar could not quite hold the ball as he dived at forward short-leg. In that close catching position, Solkar was more than a fieldsman, more than a catcher: he was another sharp prong in the attack. Wadekar had flung a tight net around the batsmen; D'Oliveira had got through that net, to find a handful of exciting runs, but was then picked up elsewhere. Venkat, having just moved his mid-on deeper, lured D'Oliveira to a lofted shot which was skied and well held by substitute Jayantilal. England were 49 for 4 and relying heavily on Luckhurst, playing a typically phlegmatic innings. And, of course, they were relying again on Alan Knott, enjoying a truly Indian summer with the bat.

Knott faced only two balls of the next 20 before he faced Venkat for the first time. He prodded the ball sufficiently off the ground for Solkar to throw himself almost on to the popping crease to make the catch. The Indians' relief was as great as their joy. Illingworth was in at 54 for 5. Not the best of players again leg-spin, though a great survivor, this time he survived several alarms in not many minutes – including one chance – before he returned a slower ball to Chandra. England, 65 for 6, were just 136 ahead, at mid-afternoon on the fourth day.

Was Luckhurst going to save his side? It would be a nice twist if he did, and not untypical of the patient, pragmatic professional. His previous experience for England at The Oval had produced a pair of ducks and, though he had made yet another duck in the first innings of this match, he had started the second with no obvious anxiety: ready as always to try to contribute, ready to accept dismissal if the ball was again good enough. He had 'read' and played the off-spinner in a consistently competent manner, and contrived to keep out Chandra more successfully than others, when on 32 – out of England's 72 for 6 – his restraint cracked and he slashed to slip.

This time there had been no recovery, nor would there be against slow bowlers who had found their rhythm on a pitch that was much to their liking. Underwood lasted uneasily with Hutton for nine overs. Then Bedi came to rest Chandra, got Underwood out on the sweep-shot in that over; and then Chandra returned immediately to wind it up, which he did by claiming Price lbw. England's second innings had lasted just two and a half hours. The total of 101 was their lowest against India by some 30 runs; it was their lowest at home against any opponents since 1948 when the Australians shot them out for 52 here at The Oval. There was no devil in the wicket to be held responsible, and the batting, though unimpressive, was far from irresponsible. The cause was splendid bowling from, especially, the wrist-spin of Chandra, and also from the finger-spin of Venkat – each of them, on the same slow wicket, gaining consistently more bounce and turn than their respective counterparts, Underwood and Illingworth.

So India, who hours previously had been bracing themselves against the prospect of an English offensive, now needed just 173 runs to win, with all the time they cared to take. Yet the task was by no means an easy one. A country who were yet to win a Test match in England in 39 years, would have any self-doubt cruelly exploited by pressure from Illingworth's men. India faced a post-tea session of two and a quarter hours as Gavaskar and Mankad went to the wicket. Gavaskar was the most important of figures in the Indian line-up, following his series in the West Indies where in four Tests he compiled 774 runs at an average of 154. His partner, Mankad, had experienced a wretched series, looking out of his depth as he struggled even to make double figures. Now it was Gavaskar who fell almost immediately, in Snow's second over, playing no stroke at a ball which straightened. He was plainly lbw and he knew it, as he walked dejectedly out.

Illingworth's men had rather easily opened up an early crack. But Mankad, who seemed to pose them no threat, was not as easily dismissed. Again, he looked to be struggling, at least by comparison with the authoritative Wadekar; but he did not in fact play many false strokes, and to England's growing concern he 'hung about'. Snow and Price were bowled for only five overs each on this very slow wicket, for Illingworth and Underwood to bowl almost through to the end of the day. It was a crucial session. And vital was the role that Mankad played as, though he scored only 11 runs, he played 74 balls, lasted for an hour and a quarter, and helped Wadekar take the score up to 37. Small figures, maybe, but with the pressure on early, and a target of only 173, it was a most valuable contribution.

At 37 for 2 and an hour to play Sardesai joined Wadekar. The next five overs produced just one run. Then Wadekar, on 22, swung at Underwood. The ball ballooned behind Knott, and as the players shouted 'catch' Edrich ran around from backward square-leg to take it. Wadekar stayed his ground; umpire Elliott, evidently uncertain, allowed that the ball may have come off the body and ruled 'not out'. It was a decision of great importance, not pleasing the fielding side. Certainly it heightened the tension. In the same over Wadekar took a four, in the next over Sardesai got off the mark and the runs began to trickle again. Throughout the final three-quarters of an hour they were coming steadily, with some clean shot-making, and at the close India were 76 for 2, with Wadekar on 45 and Sardesai on 13. Underwood had bowled 15 overs for 25 and one wicket, Illingworth 12 overs for 15 and no wicket. Thousands of miles away, traffic had halted in the streets of Bombay as crowds gathered to listen to the radio commentary.

Even with less than 100 to make and eight wickets left, India still had much to do. The prospect of a couple of wickets falling together was their fear, and it was Illingworth's hope. In fact one went down straight away, and needlessly. The batsman with the runs, on whom India so heavily depended, the man whose nerves were by far the soundest – captain

Wadekar – was run out in the day's second over, when, after hesitating over a run to short third man, he failed by a fraction to beat D'Oliveira's throw.

Viswanath joined Sardesai with India three wickets now against the overnight score of 76. In the next half hour, against Underwood and Illingworth, they added just 11 runs from 11 overs, eight of them maidens. Little Viswanath started with a single around the corner. Twenty balls later his next scoring stroke was a cut that flew past the hands of Hutton at slip. Sardesai meanwhile was adding just four runs to his overnight three. Illingworth continued to surround both batsmen with catching fieldsmen – for Viswanath, four on the off side almost within arm's length. But the batsmen accepted, and played, the game of attrition. One single in an over, or every second over, was all right for them. And once in a while, on the law of averages, a loose ball would have to be bowled. Sardesai seized on one when he straight-drove Underwood for four, and another when he stroked Snow wide of mid-off for three.

Snow bowled only six overs and Price none at all; attempts at bouncers were quite wasted on this slowest of wickets. The spinners were again in tandem as India approached lunch, as Viswanath and Sardesai approached a 50 partnership (having played 19 maidens in 34 overs); and, with a four to Sardesai taking the total up to 124, India came to within 50 runs. Then Underwood at last got a ball to turn, and Knott reacted brilliantly with an acrobatic right-handed catch.

In a further 20 minutes, 10 runs had been added, when Solkar drove at Underwood who stuck out a left hand to hold the catch. At 134 for 5 the match was still not won. Illingworth knew that if he could send back Engineer straightaway the biggest crack of all would have been made, allowing that pressure to sweep away the Indian innings.

To Underwood's first ball, Engineer aimed a crude swing; fortunately for him the ball missed bat and wickets. In Underwood's next over Viswanath surprisingly did the same. Then they both put their heads down, and picked their way through to lunch. The total was now 146 for 5. Just 70 runs had been scored in the two-and-a-half-hour session. Viswanath's 29, which was chanceless, contained no boundary – nor was his innings to in its ultimate course of nearly three hours.

After lunch Engineer was quick to force from the back foot. A heady six runs – a pulled two and a four behind point – came in Underwood's next over. It was the biggest gain from any one over so far in the day – though now, with India into the last 15 runs, and Luckhurst being given the ball, Engineer twice more swung fours to leg. India were galloping now, Viswanath let go the reins – swung cross-batted for the boundary that would do it, and nicked to Knott. No matter. Abid Ali came in and finished it off in the same over, with a square-cut four that was swept up by the oncoming crowd. All of London's Indians, it seemed, took to the field to garland their heroes. The mood was hardly one of wild excitement, more of happiness and pride. For them, life in the foreign metropolis was most probably now several degrees better.

England, of course, had not surrendered easily. The final day occupied three hours, and 60 overs, as India made their final 98 runs. Illingworth bowled in all 36 overs for 40 runs: but no wickets.

N. H.

MOUNTAINS AND MOLEHILLS

Victoria v New South Wales, December 1926

When England were dismissed for 52 by Australia in The Oval Test match of 1948 it was remarked that there could never have been a more bizarre contrast than between this débâcle and England's 903 for 7 declared on the same ground, also against Australia, 10 years earlier. Yet there was a near-parallel during the 1926–27 season in Australia – of two Sheffield Shield matches between Victoria and New South Wales, only one month apart, when Victoria's score in the first match was over a thousand – yes, one thousand! – more than their first innings in the return match.

The ludicrous story began to unfold in Melbourne on Christmas Eve, 1926. The young New South Wales team, missing the services of big names such as Herbie Collins, Warren Bardsley, Charlie Macartney, Johnny Taylor, Jack Gregory, Bert Oldfield, and Charlie Kelleway for a variety of reasons, went into the match against Victoria in good heart, having just made 446 in the fourth innings to defeat South Australia at Adelaide. Their skipper was Alan Kippax, who had scored four centuries in five innings up to the Adelaide match (including an unbeaten 271 in his final match of the previous season, making nonsense of the selectors' decision not to include him in the team to tour England in 1926). They had beaten Queensland in a remarkable opening match in which only eight runs separated the sides after 1502 runs had been scored in four days. That was in Brisbane. In Sydney the Queenslanders, new to Sheffield Shield cricket, got their own back, winning by five wickets. Then came the victory at Adelaide – reward for dedication and courage. 'Kippax's Lads' held their heads high.

By the end of the Victoria match it was all they could do to raise a smile.

Batting first on a good wicket, New South Wales were all out by five o'clock for 221. Several batsmen got started only to find a way of getting out. Kippax himself was out of form, taking 97 minutes to score 36; he was one batsman with an excuse for getting out – a shooter from Liddicut hit the base of his stumps. Norman Phillips made 52 before square-cutting into the large hands of 44-year-old Don Blackie. Tommy Andrews, one of only three experienced men in the side, was stumped off leg-spinner Hartkopf, and young University student Jim Hogg was left 40 not out. Arthur Liddicut, the opening bowler, took the main bowling honours, 4 for 50, for once bowling not so much wide of the off stump as at the wicket, albeit off stump. Jack Ryder, the medium-pace trundler, took 3 for 32, off-spinner Blackie 2 for 34. Victoria nurtured hopes of a sizable first-innings lead.

By the time their first wicket fell they were actually 154 runs ahead! Bill Woodfull – the first to be dismissed, for 133 – and Bill Ponsford posted 375 for the first wicket in only three hours and three-quarters, a Sheffield Shield record, and a reminder from Ponsford of what an insatiable appetite for runs he possessed. He had begun the season with 214 and 54 against South Australia, and a week earlier, in his second State match of the season, he took 151 off Queensland. Four years previously he had made 429 – a world record individual score – in Victoria's 1059 (also a world record) against Tasmania at Melbourne. That was in 1922–23. In 1927–28 he was to embark upon an astounding sequence of 133, 437, 202, 38, and 336. If there had been no Bradman, Ponsford's is the name that would spring to the lips of any cricketer wishing to draw comparisons with the greatest acquirer of runs.

Ponsford's style did not please everyone. He was not exactly all grace, but he played the slow spinners with clinically precise footwork, driving with a heavy bat either side of the bowler, less often through the covers. He cut immaculately, and, like all masters of the trade of run-getting, knew all about placement. Even when fieldsmen congregated in his favourite areas he was often able to toy with them by playing towards them softly for a single, then drawing them in so close that they were powerless to cut off his firmly-struck drive.

In this huge partnership with Woodfull, Ponsford made almost two runs to his partner's one, reaching his century in 125 minutes, 200 in 203 minutes and 300 in 285 minutes. By the end of the day he was 334 not out, just 31 short of Clem

Hill's Sheffield Shield record of 365 not out, set 26 years earlier at Adelaide.

Ponsford's partner for the second wicket was the lanky all-rounder H. S. T. L. 'Stork' Hendry, who, having got a sight of the ball, began to hit with abandon, not caring all that much if he should be caught: his big hits kept eluding fieldsmen and crashing into the palings and over into the crowd. Woodfull had escaped a run-out when still in double-figures, and now Hendry had some luck, being missed at six. The second-wicket stand stormed on, and Victoria finished the second day a phenomenal 573 for one wicket. Hendry's contribution to the stand of 198 in only 97 minutes was 86 not out. The New South Wales bowlers and fielders lingered under the showers and looked forward to a good night's sleep.

Next morning Ponsford reached 350 and acknowledged the crowd's applause for another 50 for the seventh time. Hill's record was just a few minutes away. Then, to 25,000 groans, he hit outside a ball from Morgan and nicked it into his stumps. He was out for 352, bemoaning his 'bad luck' as he unbuckled his pads. The second wicket had been worth 219.

Now tall Jack Ryder came in, and if the toiling New South Welshmen felt the tide was turning, they were to watch even more than Ponsford's 36 boundaries from the bat of the Victorian skipper. Using the long handle, Ryder drove with enormous power, sometimes stepping out to the ball, other times waiting for it to pitch and then belting it with a full swing of the bat. With these drives and a savage pull to anything short he roared to a century in 115 minutes, to 150 in 147 minutes, and an hour and a quarter later he was 250. Having lost Hendry almost as soon as he came in (caught at slip off the tireless Mailey for 100 in 113 minutes), Ryder, with over 600 runs on the huge and explanatory Melbourne scoreboard, felt no real anxiety as Love and King were soon both stumped by Andy Ratcliffe off Mailey. The 'collapse' to 657 for 5 was soon steadied!

Hartkopf (61) stayed with Ryder while 177 runs were added for the sixth wicket, and when Mailey, Australia's prodigal leg-spin/googly bowler, who had bowled on and on into the breeze, picked up his fourth wicket in Hartkopf, this let in Liddicut, who saw Ryder's thunderous assault continue. The 800 had come up in six hours, and the mountainous records by each State topped one after the other. Just after Liddicut's departure, bowled by McGuirk, the Sheffield Shield record of 918 (New South Wales v South Australia at Sydney, 1901) was broken. Jack Ellis, Victoria's ebullient wicket-keeper, was in now, and to him fell the honour of making the one-thousandth run, which he completed waving his bat wildly and shouting 'Long live Victoria!'

Mailey returned to the attack – if the bowling may be referred to as such – having already conceded over 300 runs, and Ryder deposited him into the pavilion for his fourth six. Then, after batting for 245 minutes for his 295, the hefty Victorian mis-hit Andrews to mid-on, where Kippax gratefully held the catch. It was now 1043 for 8, and the world record total was a mere 16 runs away. Three runs later Frank Morton was run out without scoring, and last man Blackie, destined to make his Test debut in two years' time when in his 47th year, walked out to join an excited Ellis. Every stroke was cheered, until Ellis finally played his favourite square cut behind point off Andrews and the batsmen ran to take the total to 1061. Ellis repeated his 'Long live Victoria!' act.

The 1100 was passed, and at last, after an unprecedented innings stretched over 10 and a half hours, Victoria were all out for 1107 when Ellis was run out for 63. To the last the New South Wales colts had fielded keenly, inspired by the perpetual high standard of 'Tosser' Andrews at cover-point. Ratcliffe, despite several costly misses, kept wicket diligently, and after his marathon 64 overs Arthur Mailey could still smile, saying that it was a pity that Ellis was run out, for he was just finding a length. His figures of 4 for 362 would have been improved, he ruefully remarked, if a chap in a tweed coat hadn't dropped Ryder in the shilling stand! When he jokingly asked Ponsford if his bat was within the regulation $4\frac{1}{4}$-inch width, the batsman said, 'You ought to know. You've been looking at it long enough!'

Going in again an absurd 886 runs in arrears, New South Wales put together 230 and lost by an innings and 656 runs. Ratcliffe, moving from behind the stumps, where he had seen more runs made in a single innings than any 'keeper before (or since), enjoyed making 44 of his own, and the 17-year-old Archie Jackson, before whom lay a highly successful but tragically brief future, was left not out 59. Hartkopf and Liddicut shared the wickets, and the crowd went home, proud at having been present, but, the majority of them, feeling that this sort of thing was hardly cricket at its best.

If they wanted lower scoring they needed to have been in Sydney a month later when Victoria played the return match. This time they were without Woodfull, Ponsford, and Ryder, who had accounted for 780 of Victoria's 1107 runs, and wicket-keeper Love and leg-spinner Hartkopf were missing. Another major difference was that, having taken first innings, New South Wales amassed 469 – more like a winning total – and the graceful, wristy Alan Kippax returned to his best form with a delightful 217 not out, made in under four hours.

Victoria had the ill-luck to bat on a rain-affected pitch, and only Davie, 10 not out, reached double-figures. The destroyers on that helpful pitch were Ray McNamee, fast-medium right-arm, who brought the ball back from the off. He took 7 for 21, and actually had 6 for 11 when Victoria were staggering at 19 for eight wickets. Macartney, back in the side in his final season of big cricket, and better remembered for his dynamic batting, reminded the cricket world of his ability as a left-arm spinner, particularly before the First World War, by taking the other three wickets for 10. Victoria all out 35. It seemed like a cricketing fantasy, but to those New South Wales players who had slogged and slaved on the Melbourne Cricket Ground in December it was a sweet experience.

Victoria made 181 in the follow-on, and lost by an innings and 253 runs on the third day, and a week later, with Ponsford back and making another century, they demonstrated their capricious nature once more against Queensland at Brisbane, scoring 86 in the first innings and 518 in the second, when only 753 would have been enough to win the match. That defeat was to cost them the Sheffield Shield. That roller-coaster season's performance was to make them a conversation topic for years to come.

A. T.

G.M.T.

Northamptonshire v The New Zealanders, Northampton, May 1973

From the county ground at Northampton the cricket writer for a national newspaper, on the 'phone to his office, was getting a little irritated with his editor's queries. A cricketer stood on the brink of one of the game's most coveted achievements, a thousand runs before the end of May, and the sports editor's cross-examination seemed almost to suggest doubts that the circumstances were real or valid. 'Well', said the writer, 'he's been around for several seasons, he's matured and steadily improved . . .' In a sense, however, the editor's puzzlement was understandable.

Glenn Turner, a young opening batsman from New Zealand, had made regular hundreds for Worcestershire (including a county record of 10 in a season) and played some very long innings in Test matches, twice carrying his bat: but to a distant observer his name did not seem to have resounded around the land like that of Bradman or Hammond. Men who offer great deeds are expected to possess names which ring in the mind, they are supposed to dominate the stage like great actors, and certainly they must *look* like men and not boys. Glenn Turner, even at 25 and with fashionably long hair protruding from under his cap, still looked extraordinarily youthful with his boyish face, slender arms, and thin wrists. Indeed, at a distance he looked not unlike a schoolboy. This was the batsman who, as May 1973 ended, was threatening to do what no one had done since before the War, to join the six men (Grace, Hayward, Hammond, Hallows, Bradman, and Bill Edrich) who had scored the Thousand before the end of May.

On closer inspection, the youthful-looking batsman was not so improbable a claimant. His initials, G.M.T., rightly suggested exactitude and constancy of performance. His style was the complete antithesis of the solid-set, massively *effective*

Bradman. His back-lift had a pristine straightness, he played his front-foot shots *en point*, with a classically high follow-through of the elbows. He seemed to sharpen his shots, so that somehow they always looked long and pointed. The meticulous care of his stroke-play was mirrored when, fielding at slip, he fastidiously flicked and patted the turf with the toe of his boot. An intelligent mind sought to remove emotion and tension and to leave room only for calm analysis; he *always* seemed to know how and why he was out and to, so to speak, 'rationalise it away'. But the over-riding factor, especially so far as the Thousand runs was concerned, was the ability to concentrate when it really mattered. That concentration could be fierce. There was already impressive evidence of it.

During his record-breaking season for Worcestershire in 1970, he achieved his highest Championship innings of 137 on the last day of one county game and then on the very next day, in another game, improved it with an unbeaten 154. This capacity to re-summon and maintain concentration was seen again in the West Indies, this time on a formidable scale. Early in New Zealand's tour, he made the first double-century of his career, 202 in nine hours. In his next innings, in the first Test, he superseded that by carrying his bat for 223, in nine and a half hours. Later on that tour, against Guyana at Georgetown, he made 259 in 10 hours – then followed up again on the same pitch, in the Test match, by exactly repeating this 259, this time in 11 and three-quarter hours. On each of the four times he reached 100 on that tour he went on to pass 200.

So, the application was clearly there, if he wanted to seek the Thousand. Whether the target was in his mind very early in New Zealand's 1973 tour is doubtful. But it certainly arose in the public mind after he started with 41 and 151 not out in the opening match against Derrick Robins' XI and followed with 143 against Worcester – 335 runs even before April was finished. With the press continuing to record these totals, and his team selecting him for every game, there was no ignoring the target even if he wanted to. Wet weather meant fewer batting opportunities in the next three county matches and also a couple of failures. (But not as many as referred to in the 1974 *Wisden*, which included amongst all 'failures' in May two low not-out innings.) Good weather and wicket at Cardiff provided around 50 in each innings against Glamorgan, as well as reinforcing his good form. When he came to Lord's for the MCC match, starting on 19 May, the aggregate stood at 630 and needed another long innings to bring the Thousand within striking distance.

Now, like it or not, the pressure got to Turner. Batting first at Lord's, he went some 20 minutes without scoring. In that time he felt physically sick with anxiety, and wished he could quit the field. The feeling passed when the first run was scored and, in a long partnership with Parker, he proceeded to play his best innings of the summer, one which was chanceless and in which his confidence ultimately led him to hit sixes off both Birkenshaw and Underwood. At the declaration, he had 153. In another opportunity at the end of the game he was bowled with a stunning delivery from Cottam for three. Still, the target was now just 201 runs away, and he had three matches.

The following Saturday he went to the wicket at Leicester (with this match and one to follow) needing 133. The goal was large, but within reach. Such statistical goals are perhaps unnatural to cricket, and on this day Turner seemed to freeze. Against the opening bowlers he gathered runs carefully, but when the slow men appeared he came to a halt. On the Leicester wicket the ball was not coming on to the bat as he would have liked, and Birkenshaw and Balderstone did not bowl a loose ball. Had they done so, even just one, it may well have freed Turner and opened the way to the hundred. In 50 minutes after the fall of the first wicket Turner had scored only five to Congdon's 17. Then, most untypically, he played the shot of frustration, got a top edge to his sweep and was easily caught. He had taken most of the morning to make 30. 'It's funny', he confessed at lunchtime. 'It's the first time I can ever remember that, as the bowler was running up, I was thinking, "This ball could get me out".' Subsequently, Congdon went on to get such a score as Turner needed, 134. In the second innings, Turned was 10 overnight, only to see the final day rained out.

He had, it seemed, left it too late. The next game, against Northamptonshire, would be played on 30, 31 May and 1 June. With two days of the match before May ended, New Zealand would have to bat first if Turner was to have any chance of two innings; more likely he would have just one. The pressure was too great now, to have to go out and make the 93 necessary runs in one innings. Additionally, it looked as if the pitch would be wet. But if any batsman could bat on such a knife-edge as this, and make the prescribed runs, here was one with the mental capacity.

The rain which had ruined the last day at Leicester continued into the night and made the following morning damp, though clear enough. The wicket that had been prepared looked as if it would be especially slow to improve, and another was cut on the other side of the square. While cosmetic work was done on the rest of the square, and a mid-afternoon start anticipated, Turner marshalled the autograph hunters who threatened to besiege him. Sitting on a seat by the pavilion railings he patiently signed his way through a queue of boys which stretched some 50 yards out into the field. Northants won the toss and put New Zealand in. Turner was afterwards to describe the wicket as 'dangerous', a forthright description for a rational mind not usually given to dramatisation.

Play began at half-past three under cloudy skies. Against Dye the left-armer and Hodgson, a tall young bowler, the batsmen began quietly. Turner was soon withdrawing his bottom hand quickly, and standing on tip-toe to play the lifting ball. He was given a bonus by a full toss from Hodgson, which he put through mid-off for four; but straightaway he edged just short of the slips, and twice cut without making contact. Dye was worrying him, and the slip fieldsmen remained in a state of anticipation. With 12 on the board, his partner Parker was lbw to Dye. Congdon came in and was soon taking the ball on the body. On 16, Turner went for the off-drive against Dye and the ball nicked down into the slips. Low on his left hand, Virgin at first slip could not hold it.

Play to tea had been little more than survival for the batsmen. But afterwards Turner began to make rapid progress. Against Dye he twice played handsome square-cuts to the boundary. He seemed to relish these shots, and now he had the confidence to steer the ball down to third man for singles – risky, perhaps, but his judgment was sure. Soon enough the attack was joined by the turbaned Bedi, the best slow left-arm bowler in the world. An unnerving prospect, except that Turner normally enjoys playing slow bowlers. He soon square-cut Bedi for four, and then square-drove him for another. They were both speciality strokes, the first clipped away from very close to the body, the second more of a 'flat-bat' to a ball of more width and fuller length, both of them potentially hazardous strokes but played with emphatic confidence. The second took him to his 50 – with the rush after tea, scored in only 90 minutes. It was now 10 minutes past five. He had another 80 minutes to go on to 93.

Then, with a bold and less typical stroke, he swept Bedi for four – and then tried it again, and missed. Perhaps this worried him. A few months before, in a Test series in New Zealand against Pakistan, he was out three times in five dismissals to the leg-spin of Intikhab, each time to the sweep. It had also got him out at Leicester. And now when he also played and missed at Willey, he reined in his strokes. At the other end Congdon took up the shot-making, and the larger part of the strike. Sheltering Turner he may have been; more likely he was just playing, as always, as well as he possibly could whatever the circumstances. Contrivance so often leads astray the best laid plans. Near the end of the day Congdon even took a sharp single to cover, which had Turner scampering. So Turner added just 15 in the last hour, and ended the day on 70. Was his conservatism in the last hour a loss of nerve? Or was it a sign of strong nerve that he was prepared to wait, and give himself 23 more runs to make in the morning? Certainly it was now quite obvious that there would be no second innings for him before the end of the second day.

At least, the weather had held when play resumed the next morning – but only just, for the cool grey skies threatened light rain. Twenty-three runs, it seemed, could be knocked off in a few overs. But they were not. The bowling was taken up again by Dye and Hodgson. Turner now would not be beaten by either, but the only runs he could score were singles down to third man: he gained just three in the half hour. Twenty runs seemed a long way off, the tension great. Photographers and television cameramen waited – prepared to have nothing, after all, to report. With the clock just past mid-day, Hodgson dropped one short and Turner seized on it, square-cutting for four to take him to 79.

Now Bedi came on. In this situation his bowling could be expected to be as un-erring as Turner's concentration; and it was. The period of play which followed, on this modest county ground, was of an excellence scarcely matched at any level of cricket. Turner as usual elected to play most deliveries, as indeed he had to. Once, Bedi got one to jump past the defensive stroke. Once, Turner moved down the wicket to him and cover-drove through Larkins at cover for four. The continuity of the drama was broken as, at the other end, Congdon mistimed a pull to short mid-wicket and walked out for 72, having added 17 this morning to Turner's 14, and contributed to a partnership worth 154. There was further distraction when Turner, backing-up, started for a run only to have to dive back to safety as Milburn made a good stop and return. Otherwise, all the play seemed to crystallise on Bedi curving the ball through the air, to be met by Turner's straight bat dropping the ball in front of him or pushing it calmly and firmly down to mid-off – while he waited, and waited, for the one that was dropped a fraction shorter...

Bedi had been bowling for half an hour, and Turner in all the first hour had gone from 70 to 85. Then the bat flashed at an off-stump ball, which went with a pistol crack to the boundary behind point. It was the speciality shot, played to a ball which is really much too close to the body (and off stump) and not short enough for square-cutting, a ball which other batsmen might start to play and then leave – or, if they did flash at it, would be likely to snick. But Turner, positioned with weight spread equally between front and back foot, watching it with an eagle eye, tucks in tight on it and, almost off his right hip bone, flashes it away. A 'slash' for want of a better term, but propelled with the speed and certainty of a bullet.

It is not a bad ball, a loose ball, from which Bedi has been hit for four. He will not be blaming himself. But does he bowl it again? Does he tempt the batsman to repeat the risk, or does he avoid the batsman's strength? He starts a new over, with Turner on 89, wanting one boundary. This time each of the six balls is played with the straight face of the bat, or left. The tension is acute, heightened by the cameras trained on every ball of the maiden over.

At a quarter to one, Bedi bowls again to Turner ... Again the front foot goes forward, the weight suddenly shifts back again, the eagle eye follows the crack of the bat and the ball rifling away to the backward-point fence.

The clapping spectators, and the players who run forward to offer warm congratulation, seem more relieved and pleased than the batsman. Still, the innings certainly changes gear as he goes in carefree style to his hundred, reaching it with a four snicked past slip, and finally hits a towering off-drive to be caught for 111 – rightly enough, off Bedi.

Afterwards, he maintains that he has tried to disallow himself feelings of satisfaction, and when television interviewers want to know his 'secret' he tells the BBC and a bemused audience of millions: 'Well, most batsmen tend to play either from the front foot or the back foot, and to play either the line or the length; and I suppose, basically, I am a front-foot, line player.'

N. H.

COMETH THE HOUR

South Africa v England, Durban, December 1948

'Cometh the hour, cometh the man!' Thus spake, according to legend, Clifford Gladwin, fast bowler for Derbyshire and England, and his country's number 10 in the crisis of the closing overs of one of the most thrilling of Test matches.

England had had slightly the better of the play throughout the four days of this the first Test of the 1948–49 series in South Africa, but with 13 runs wanted in 13 minutes the seventh wicket fell – the important wicket of Denis Compton – and two runs later another England wicket went. Any of the four possible results – win, loss, draw, or tie – was likely as Gladwin strode out to join another big Englishman who rightfully batted in the lower half of the order: Alec Bedser. The remaining minutes were frantic, wretched, heroic, memorable.

F. G. Mann was leading England in his first Test match, and with a good-looking Kingsmead pitch beckoning and turbulent weather in the offing, he called 'heads' in the hope of gaining first use of the wicket. The coin fell tails-up, and Dudley Nourse eagerly seized first innings for South Africa. A few hours later his side had lost the initiative in the face of some superb swing bowling and marvellous fielding.

Eric Rowan, recalled to the side in his 40th year, was the first to go – not to pace but to Roly Jenkins' leg-break (only his third ball in Test cricket), which he edged to 'keeper Evans in a desperate attempt at a late-cut after advancing down the pitch. With the total only 18, Wynne was adeptly caught by Compton at backward short-leg off Bedser, and then came resistance from two great South African batsmen, Bruce Mitchell and Dudley Nourse. Mitchell was his usual intractable self, but Nourse was beginning to look dangerous, opening up against the awkward bowling. They had added 51 for the third wicket when an astonishing catch reversed fortunes. Nourse played

Wright, the medium-pace leg-spinner, just forward of square-leg, but Allan Watkins, the rotund little Glamorgan all-rounder, dived to his right (his 'wrong' side) and clasped the catch about an inch from the ground. Bowlers and fielders were inspired anew.

Apart from one period of resistance – a sixth-wicket stand of 49 – this marked the beginning of a downward slide to the innings. Billy Wade, next man in, had made only eight when a brilliant throw by Washbrook square-on at cover broke the wicket to run him out. Begbie equalled Nourse's top score for the innings (37), but another slick catch by Compton, two further catches by Evans, and some skilful bowling in the thundery atmosphere by Bedser and Gladwin reduced South Africa to 161 all out.

Hutton and Washbrook had time only to put England's first run on the board when rain began to fall heavily and the light became impossible. The batsmen were booed by the crowd for their lack of consideration in appealing, but the umpires saw it their way with less than one full over bowled. It had been, after all, a day for fielders and bowlers: Bedser 4 for 39, Gladwin 3 for 21.

The second day saw England reach a commanding position, yet time seemed now to be the enemy. Less than three hours' play was possible on the Friday, England reaching 144 for 2, but with two days remaining it seemed that if there was to be an outright result then there would need to be some penetrative bowling. Would the pitch encourage this? It seemed a distinct possibility with all the rain about. Indeed, Athol Rowan, the off-spinner, and 'Tufty' Mann, the left-arm spinner, were already getting some turn before torrential rain ended play for the day. The pitch was covered with tarpaulin sheets, and was drenched. If strong sun should beam upon it it could become a nightmare to bat on. While the going was reasonably good on that second day, Len Hutton had batted coolly and expertly for 81 not out, and Compton, who had thrashed 300 in three hours off North-Eastern Transvaal a fortnight earlier, was with him. Washbrook (35) and Reg Simpson (five in his initial Test innings) were gone. There was much expectancy as the third day's play began.

There was a background drama to the third day. With all the rain about, Mann, England's skipper, visited the ground at dawn and spoke with the groundsman, who confirmed his belief that the longer the rolling of the pitch was delayed the more difficult it would become for batting. The seven minutes' rolling could be carried out at any time after midnight before play was due to begin. The sun was now starting to grill the earth, and an early rolling would probably have resulted in a fine batting wicket. Left till later, it would crack and crumble the baked surface. Mann plumped for the latter course, and this was to decide the match.

Twelve wickets fell for 199 runs for the delectation of Saturday's crowd. Compton almost fell to the first ball. That would have lost England the match. He went on to a 72 that was worth practically any of his many centuries, deftly holding off Mann and Rowan, who bowled throughout the rest of England's innings. The early dismissal of Hutton for 83 gave the Springboks a lift, but while Compton was in there was an obstacle to their hopes. Against the spinning and lifting ball he was master, letting runs come, not forcing them, as was his nature. His footwork time and again got him out of trouble, and when eventually the persistent 'Tufty' Mann had him caught he had held fast for 212 minutes, hitting only four fours.

George Mann, with 19, was the only other England batsman to show any signs of coping, and England had to make do with a lead of 92. 'Tufty' Mann's stamina and low-trajectory accuracy were rewarded with 6 for 59 off 37.4 eight-ball overs of which 14 were maidens. He was to finish top of South Africa's averages in the series with 17 wickets at 25.29, but after his second tour of England, in 1951, he was to be forced out of the game with a terminal illness. One of the most economical bowlers of any type in cricket history, Mann died in 1952 at the tragically early age of 30.

Athol Rowan, the off-spinner, who bowled even more overs – 44 – than Mann, took 4 for 108. England's spinners, sitting in the dressing-room and then having their own look at the pitch during their brief innings, must have suffered itchy fingers.

Their turn came. By the end of the third day, when bad light had yet again curtailed play, South Africa were uncomfortably placed at 90 for 4 – still two runs behind. Eric Rowan, Wynne, Mitchell, and Nourse were all out, and the odds were heavily on England, with further weather interference the only hazard.

Billy Wade and Denis Begbie had other ideas. With brave and judicious batsmanship they added 85 runs for South Africa's fifth wicket in 82 minutes, and suddenly the match seemed to be fading into the draw which many thought inevitable when so much rain cascaded down over the first three days. The cynics are always willing to write off a cricket match at the first sign of adverse mathematics: here England needed five quick wickets and then some authoritative batting. Others, knowing what a topsy-turvy game it can be, hang on until the last vestige of hope has vanished. At Durban in December 1948 that final vestige was still just visible, and the optimists were to be rewarded.

Wade's admirable 63 was ended when Jenkins spun one through him, and Begbie was caught by Mann off Bedser two short of his 50. Then there was a crash. Wright accounted for Dawson and Athol Rowan, and finished with 4 for 72, and Compton, having a rare Test match bowl, took the wicket of 'Tufty' Mann, caught by England's George Mann – prompting John Arlott, who was giving radio commentary, to remark upon 'Mann's inhumanity to Mann'! When Jenkins, who finished with 3 for 64, wrapped up the innings by bowling last man McCarthy, South Africa had managed only 219, and the calculations began.

England had a possible 135 minutes' batting time and the total required for victory was 128. F. G. Mann soon made it known to everyone in the England dressing-room that they were to go after the runs. It would undoubtedly call for risks to be taken, but there was to be no hesitation.

Washbrook hit a catch to Wynne on the leg boundary off Tuckett's first ball, but the fieldsman could not hold the greasy ball, and the spectators groaned. Then a square cut off McCarthy by the same batsman hit Nourse in the gully a crunching blow on the knee, and a precious five minutes were lost. Some felt the fieldsman should have left the field, but eventually he resumed, and the next frustration was a sharp shower which caused a delay of 12 minutes. Any urgency felt at the start of the innings was now doubled.

Then the wickets began to tumble. Hutton, the great Hutton, was caught at short-leg off Lindsay Tuckett; then Washbrook was leg-before to Mann, and it was 49 for 2. George Mann, who had raised himself to number three in the order, was missed twice as the gloom made catching almost as difficult as batting. Cuan McCarthy, the young, blond fast bowler, who was to be no-balled for throwing before his brief and spectacular career was over, had Mann magnificently caught in the slips by Mitchell, and it was 52 for 3. With drizzle drifting down and the light appalling, with the tension mounting by the minute, and with the ball slippery to the grip, the 19-year-old from Pietermaritzburg was to bowl through the remainder of this eventful innings.

Watkins, having made only four, was bowled by McCarthy, and Simpson was caught first ball: 64 for 5. Six runs later Evans, after skipping a few hectic singles, was also bowled by McCarthy, and England were in trouble. An hour remained, and 58 runs were needed. The England dressing-room door was locked, and players who could not bear to watch the action paced up and down. Compton, the first-innings hero, carried most of England's hopes and aspirations. With him was the merry Jenkins of Worcestershire. An appeal against the awful conditions would certainly have been upheld, but such action was unthinkable.

The batsmen fought, stealing a single here, a two there. Compton, the last recognised batsman, did his best to shield his partner from the strike, though runs were not to be eschewed.

They took England to the hundred – an encouraging milestone. The total reached 115 – just 13 to get. Then McCarthy did the trick. He bowled Compton for 28, and the pressure was back on England – heavily. It was 10 minutes to six by the clock. Alec Bedser hurried out to the darkness of the middle. Two runs later Jenkins slashed at McCarthy and was given out caught behind. Cliff Gladwin, known as 'The Gaffer', came in, last man but one. Through the murk his grin was discernible, and it was Nourse at short-leg who enquired politely what he had to look so composed about. In pure Derbyshire tones, Gladwin declared 'Cometh the hour, cometh the man'. Seconds later the man was almost gone like yesterday's news. He lofted the ball to mid-on, Tuckett, who misjudged its flight in the mist, and the batsmen ran two. Another single, and Bedser, who had narrowly avoided being run out, prepared to face the final over of the match. Eight runs were wanted, and Lindsay Tuckett, who had supported McCarthy well without being as hostile, was called upon to bowl. Nourse instructed him to bowl at the stumps – for better or worse.

The field was set carefully, with Eric Rowan guarding the deep mid-wicket boundary, where any tail-ender was likely to hoist the ball. Bedser failed to make contact with the first ball, but they scrambled a leg-bye. Seven needed off seven balls. Tuckett had a lot on his mind – including the urgent necessity to keep his rear foot behind the crease, thus averting a no-ball and a free hit. He bowled to Gladwin. The batsman put all his considerable power into a cross-batted heave in the general direction of mid-on. The ball climbed and carried a great distance; Rowan, alert for the catch, ran forward from his post out near the boundary; but the ball kept carrying, and to his grief he saw it pass over his head, bounce, and run into the boundary for four runs. That surely had won the match for England? Even if Rowan had stayed out and still dropped the catch, three runs would probably have been saved.

Yet the third ball brought only one leg-bye, and Bedser failed to score off the fourth and fifth. Still all four results were possible. Tuckett ran in and bowled his sixth ball, and Bedser stabbed it into the covers and bolted a single. The scores were level.

The batsmen conferred in mid-wicket. Wade, South Africa's wicket-keeper, was standing some distance behind the stumps, and it was decided to run whatever happened to the seventh ball. It came, and Gladwin aimed the winning hit . . . and missed. Bedser started off for a leg-bye, the run that would bring England a sensational victory. But Gladwin stood transfixed, and shouted to his partner to get back. Bedser reversed his great bulk and made it safely into his ground.

One ball left. Tuckett looked to his skipper: 'What now?' Nourse told him tersely to bowl at the wicket. He did – leg-stump, but slightly short of a length, so that the ball smacked Gladwin loudly on the thigh. Off sailed the batsmen; no hesitation this time. 'Tufty' Mann pounced in from short-leg and gathered the ball, which had landed only a yard or two from the batsman. Bedser and Gladwin hurtled towards their respective ends as if the devil himself were making chase. They made it. Gladwin was leaping about, waving his bat, and hundreds were running out to the centre. England by two wickets, but cricket by a landslide!

Gladwin and the South African hero in defeat, Cuan McCarthy, were chaired off, and the jubilation lasted for hours, though the South Africans had a silent, stunned five minutes in their dressing-room before going *en masse* to the England room for handshakes and champagne all round.

Cliff Gladwin's thigh bruise was his proudest possession, something he would have liked to retain for the rest of his life. It was photographed, but faded in time. The memory of those frenetic closing moments lasted, and bids fair to immortality.

A year later Alex Bannister of the *Daily Mail* went to see Gladwin at a party in Chesterfield to celebrate the Leg-bye Victory, and the bowler-turned-matchwinning-batsman, a boilersmith and storekeeper at Doe Lea pit, recalled on that first anniversary how he had called down the pitch to Bedser, 'Don't worry, my little champion – we're going to get 'em.' He admitted it was a false bravery. 'My thoughts as I ran? Well, strangely enough, of what the Derbyshire team would think, and the boys at the pit where I worked: and as the crowd surged on to the ground and carried me aloft, my whole cricketing career raced through my brain.'

The second, third, and fourth Tests were drawn, with Hutton and Washbrook putting on a record 359 for the first wicket at Johannesburg in the second, and at Port Elizabeth, in the final Test, there was a conclusion almost as exciting as that at Durban in the first. Jack Crapp saw England home by three wickets by hitting 10 runs off three balls with only a minute left for play. England's 174 was achieved in only 95 minutes, and notably South Africa's bowlers sent down 24 eight-ball overs (all but one ball) in that time. This was the spirit of the game.

Gladwin was almost in at the death in this match too, but was dismissed for 15 when 20 runs were still required. He had already received, figuratively, the freedom of Durban. That was enough for any man whose thigh was more effective than his bat!

A. T.

THE LONGEST DAY

West Indies v Australia, World Cup Final,
Lord's, 21 June 1975

Britons crept out into the sunshine of May 1975, daring to hope for a glorious June and ready, very ready, to be disappointed. Cricket's first World Cup – a series of one-day matches for the Prudential Cup – was coming, and was it not *just* possible that it might be blessed with one of those legendary summers like '47? It was. It happened. The day before the World Cup started burst gloriously fine all over England, the anti-cyclone stayed, and in 15 matches over the course of two weeks not a minute's play was lost. The day of the final was as fine as any. The venue was Lord's and the date 21 June, the longest day. The game was one of cricket's longest, starting at 11 a.m. and ending at 8.42 p.m., and it was one of cricket's finest contests.

Lord's was sold out, filled to the corners, and could have been filled again. Perhaps half were West Indians, who had bought their seats some time in advance with a sure faith that Clive Lloyd's team would win through to this day. Australia was less well, though vociferously, represented. Englishmen (and women) and others were just as glad to be there. Few left before the finish.

Ian Chappell won the toss and asked West Indies to bat. It was the same ploy which his opponents used when they rather decisively won their group meeting a week before, bowling Australia out for 192 and then making the runs with seven wickets and many overs to spare. Often in one-day matches this tactic is justified by the pitch's having a touch of life in the morning session. This day an ideal one-day wicket had little early life, as such. But it was not heartless. From an objective standpoint, so to speak, it let bowler and batsman find their balance in an absorbing morning session.

Lillee began, as demanding as ever, to Fredericks and Greenidge, who played him correctly. At the other end Gilmour bowled three no-balls in an over that produced six runs. Thomson, the quickest of the quick, was being spared the shiny new ball he does not care to grip. It was to prove an effective arrangement. Off the last ball of Lillee's second over, Fredericks played a whirling hook to fine-leg. Six! But the shout of the crowd faded curiously as the batsman walked unhappily from the wicket. He had slipped as he pivoted – in stud-less boots – and kicked his own wicket down. After three overs: 12 for 1.

Now came Kallicharran, the little left-hander who, with shots as hard and as sharp as cut diamonds, had taken Lillee to pieces at The Oval the previous Saturday. He had also dazzled against New Zealand in the semi-final, again winning the Man of the Match award; it was being said that he was the Man of the Series. He began in such mood, soon cover-driving Gilmour for four and, after watching Greenidge play a maiden, immediately taking four more off a bouncer from Gilmour. The mood was with him still as he cut at a ball from Gilmour that was never short enough or wide enough: in fact, a ball best left. Marsh joyfully accepted the edge, and West Indies were 27 for 2 off nine overs. Lillee and Gilmour had each bowled two maidens to Greenidge – who had made just five runs, all singles, from 27 balls. And now Thomson replaced Lillee.

Thomson was immediately quick and accurate: his best performance thus far on an English visit which he had begun with a grotesque collection of no-balls and wides. Now he fully justified his Australian reputation, albeit on an English wicket offering no lift. His first over produced just a single from the last ball, his second a single from the second of two no-balls. In his third, Kanhai managed to get him away squarish to the cover boundary. Then he bowled a maiden to Greenidge, twice beating the bat. One run off the bat in his fifth over, making just seven in the five. Then he bowled again to an intense Greenidge, who had 13 runs after an hour and 20 minutes. The second ball was quick and on a perfect length near off stump. Greenidge was half-back and then half-forward, with no time to do anything else and certainly no time to adjust as the ball fractionally left him. Marsh again had the catch and Greenidge was walking off, surely without recrimination. If it was true that the ball had also kept a little low, it was the speed allied to the movement that had defeated the batsman's reflex response.

West Indies were 50 for 3 from 18 overs. With Clive Lloyd

coming in, the innings was at a crisis point. Sometimes he does not start so well, conscious of the responsibility he bears and conscious that the bowlers also are trying extremely hard at this point. This time, from the first ball, he was true to his best reputation. Thomson bowled him a good one, but he met it – not quite in the middle – with a decent swing of the bat and a show of confidence. He took a single off the next ball. His feet were moving as each ball was bowled, not in nervousness but with a sense of itching to hit the bowling. He had faced five balls when Thomson (6-1-8-1) was replaced by Lillee. The second ball of this over was smoothly dismissed in front of square-leg; the fourth, short, was lifted into the crowd behind square-leg. A single made it 11 off the over.

Lloyd was beginning a spectacular march, yet the West Indies' fortunes were by no means yet restored. With Australia continuing to press for further wickets Lillee was as hostile as ever and from the pavilion end Max Walker was hustling in with his restless medium-pace and his off-cutters biting. Kanhai had quickly appreciated the need for solidity, and at Lloyd's entry had dropped anchor: three scoring strokes only did he make from another 28 balls before lunch. Lloyd meanwhile had survived an appeal for a catch at the wicket, a slower ball from Lillee which beat him and, next ball, a chance when Edwards at short mid-wicket was evidently disconcerted by a pull stroke which was violently fashioned but mistimed; in between, however, Lloyd thumped off-side fours against Lillee, Walker, and Greg Chappell, going to lunch with 34 to Kanhai's 16, and West Indies 91 for 3 from 28 overs.

The play had been watched with rapt attention even in the non-partisan reaches of the pavilion. They had seen, especially in the hour to lunch, one of the most absorbing passages of play in international cricket.

During the interval, some of the uninitiated were inclined to ask, why is Kanhai so *slow*? To most, the importance of his role was clear, so long as runs were coming – especially so long as Lloyd was in. Probably the psychological landmark of the interval would now produce a dramatic change in the after-lunch session, as so often happens in the one-day game.

That change was not, after all, so abrupt. Kanhai continued head down, and played 14 more balls without scoring before he got Walker away to the cover boundary. Lloyd meanwhile was taking about four an over, maintaining steady but authoritative progress against Greg Chappell and the returning Thomson. Then Walker returned. Lloyd hit him first ball over his head into the pavilion fence. This gave Lloyd his 50, to Kanhai's 20. Now the senior partner at last joined in, and played a stroke against Walker which ranked with any in the day: a sumptuous stroke in which he saw a wide half-volley early and floated his weight far across to propel it like an ocean wave straight through the cover field.

The dam was beginning to break. After 35 overs the West Indies were 118 for 3. In another eight overs they had added 73, and Lloyd had his hundred. On a ground so dry that the drainage grid stood out like ribs, the ball whistled through defensive placings. The West Indies support grew increasingly noisier and animated, requiring patient discipline by a large police contingent. A long-short-short anvil rhythm tapped out on bottle and beer cans now continued as a joyful pulse-beat, accompanying spectacular action as Lloyd took Walker to pieces. He hoisted one perfectly good length ball into the Grand Stand with insolent ease – and then caressed the next ball away behind point with gorgeous timing. Poor Walker. After seven overs in the morning for 22, he had now bowled another five for 49, and scarcely bowled a loose ball. Many are the bowlers who will bowl a lot worse for greater reward than he did with his 12 overs for 71 and no wickets.

Lloyd, having gone from 50 to his hundred in exactly 10 overs, was out when umpire Bird (after discussion with Spencer at square-leg) gave him caught at the wicket to a ball from Gilmour which angled across him and went down the leg side. Lloyd, having stood his ground, seemed somewhat bemused at the decision. Still, he had benefited from some good luck, with that chance to Australia's keenest fieldsman, Ross Edwards and, on 62, an easier chance lifted towards long-leg, where Lillee ran in only to drop the ball at knee-height. The fact was that Lloyd had played an innings which did justice and more to the occasion, an innings fit for a boy's story book. The pavilion rose when he came in, an almost inadequate gesture.

Lloyd's dismissal would make little difference now. His side were 200 with 15 overs left and six wickets still to spend. For them, a happy position; for Australia a frightening one – with Richards, Boyce, and Julien next in line. In the event, they did well enough to hold the batsmen to six runs an over in the final hour. Gilmour picked up a string of wickets with his angle, his usually full-length, and his occasional slower ball. But for the West Indies spectators it was also a happy hour, as they saw Keith Boyce thrashing Thomson over mid-on for four and wicket-keeper Murray, a fine hooker, swinging Lillee square for six; and finally the popular Vanburn Holder – 'Long Tack' – coming in with two balls from Gilmour remaining, to wallop the first, one-bounce, into the long-off fence, and steal two runs off the other. The second of these two runs was given away when Walters threw unnecessarily at the bowler's stumps. A frayed ending for the Australians, whose cricketing brains must at times have felt nearly addled. Now, weary, they faced a total of 291 for 8, a winning score in anyone's book.

Of course, though, the criterion for such targets tends to be the performances of county sides in the English domestic cup competitions. What might an *international* batting order, with such as the two Chappells, Walters, and Marsh, achieve on a good wicket? And had not Pakistan, in a Prudential match against England the previous summer, scored 246 for 3 in just 43 overs?

Immediately, of course, they had to face Andy Roberts, at least Thomson's equal in speed and perhaps of more worrying accuracy. Straight away he hit McCosker's pads, made both batsmen play and miss, and his third over was a maiden. From three overs of Julien, though, the runs came a little more freely: the total was 24 from six overs when Boyce replaced Julien, and with the last ball of his first over caused McCosker to edge the out-swinger low to Kallicharran at second slip. Fortunate was Lloyd that he could rotate the attack between four bowlers such as Roberts, Julien, Boyce, and Holder. Taken together they probably aggregated a higher speed than Australia's top four. But would they prove expert at containment? Ian Chappell's initial approach, like Lloyd's earlier in the day, certainly seemed to suggest that the batsman's job was simply to overcome containment rather than to survive an attack. Julien was hooked to the square-leg boundary, off-driven for four and three. Meanwhile the left-handed Turner, an unaggressive figure, had made deceptively good progress. An exaggeratedly straight backlift – the bat disappearing behind him – seemed to contribute to one hair-raising drive against Boyce when the ball was chopped between pads and wicket and passed the wicket-keeper for four. But that poor impression was resoundingly corrected three balls later when he stepped into a similar delivery from Boyce and off-drove through to the pavilion. Chappell continued, most positive but responsible against Holder and Boyce. Runs were coming at almost exactly four an over. Overall, the required rate was nearly five, but in the period of establishment four was a highly satisfactory rate – and in fact considerably better than West Indies at the same stage.

Now, the West Indies' fifth bowler came to the crease – Lloyd himself, of modest medium-pace but the most experienced of limited-overs operators. His first ball was played by Chappell short on the on side. Chappell looked for the sort of single that needs instinctive unison between the batsmen. Turner hesitated, then perhaps got under way a little casually – as Richards picked up on the run from short mid-wicket and hit the stumps with a throw that just beat Turner's stretch for the line.

This run-out denied Australia's enjoying what was beginning to look like a handsome bonus, with Turner on 40 and almost matching Chappell, but it was surely not the worst of calamities. At 81 for 2 it brought in Greg Chappell, who played out the rest of a maiden over with typical aplomb.

Probably no-one looks better from the start than Greg Chappell. His first scoring stroke now was a four clipped away off his legs against Holder. The batsmen scarcely needed to move at this stroke, which suggested more a man going to his hundred. It must have worried the West Indies and their supporters. That same over yielded 11 in all, as Ian Chappell added a couple of drives past the bowler. In four overs to tea they added 26, and went into the interval looking well set, each of them, Ian on 42 and Greg on 14, and the total 107 for 2 from 25 overs.

Greg Chappell had just pulled a no-ball from Lloyd into the hands of Greenidge by the square-leg umpire. The more parochial West Indians down at the bottom of J stand were insisting in loud voices that the umpire had seen the ball hit, seen the catch made, and *then* raised him arm for the no-ball. Ridiculous, of course, but the irrational complaint of a few was the anxiety of many. Australia 107 for 2, and both Chappells well in. The pulse-beat rhythm of the cans and the bottles rose louder, became more insistent, as if to drive away the Australian challenge. That anxious rhythm lasted all through the tea interval, at six o'clock on an afternoon now clouded and sultry.

On the longest day, though, the light was still good as the Chappells came at a quarter past six for the match's conclusive session. Roberts returned for what would probably be another four-over burst; against New Zealand in the semi-final his second attack, after lunch, had instantly gained the two wickets necessary to kill New Zealand's challenge. Now Ian Chappell flicked a four to fine-leg in an over that produced six runs. But at the other end Lloyd had struck an awkward length, allowing no more than an occasional single. In the third over after tea, bowled by Roberts, Ian Chappell played sharply through the point area, where the ball was half stopped and there was some uncertainty between the fieldsmen Greenidge and Richards. After some stop-go hesitation the Chappells made the fateful decision to continue with the run and on the pivot Richards, again, hit the stumps, of which he could see only one, to run out Greg Chappell by a clear margin. Underlined was an old adage: 'Never run to a mis-field unless there are two runs.' Just as relevant would be to add: After uncertainty, abandon the run immediately. So, Australia were 115 for 3, in the 28th over. Ian Chappell, on the brink of his 50, was now joined by Doug Walters.

In his first over, Walters played Roberts behind the wicket for two and four, and Chappell forced him straight for three. Still, Roberts gave little else away. Lloyd continued, uncannily, only to allow singles, and had bowled seven overs for 15 when Chappell thrashed him straight for two fours down to the pavilion. Walters joined in against the returning Holder and commenced an assault which was to bring him 23 runs in four overs against that bowler. One over yielded two fours through the covers – one, the fiercest of shots from the back foot that made Holder look a medium-pacer and, with two no-balls in the same over, brought him rebuke from the West Indies spectators. Australia 162 for 3 from 38 overs. Chappell on 62 and Walters on 29. The springboard was almost set for the final 20-over rush to victory.

At seven minutes past seven, Lloyd bowled the first ball of his tenth over to Chappell, who clipped it towards mid-wicket, saw it fumbled, hesitated, and once again set out for a fateful single. This time the axe fell on him as the ball was recovered and fired perfectly to the bowler's end, where Lloyd secured the run-out as smoothly as a 'keeper. Once again the fieldsman was Richards. He had made only five runs earlier in the day but his influence on the match was now as vital as anyone's – even including that of Lloyd, who was following up his hundred with the most economical performance of all five West Indian bowlers. The run-outs of Turner and both Chappells had occurred since he started to bowl; and shortly he added another vital wicket as Walters, aiming a pull-drive, lost his off-stump, to a great shout from the stands. Of all the wickets this probably seemed the most decisive: Walters was the last good, dangerous batsman. Lloyd finished his 12 overs, bowled off the reel, for 38 runs and one wicket. Australia were 179 for 5 off 43 overs.

Edwards and Marsh were now together. The difficulty of the job was emphasised when Marsh, for whom fast scoring seems quite natural *whenever* he bats, now found it just as hard as for the diligent Edwards. In seven overs together only two shots brought more than a single, as they added 25. Then Marsh hit in frustration at Boyce and was bowled. Gilmour, an even more instinctive hitter, did a little better. But, just after he had smashed Boyce tennis-like over the top for four – raising hopes, and fears – he swung in the air to square-leg. Kanhai waited there under it, clutched it securely to his chest, and then had to scurry away to avoid being overrun by his countrymen racing on from the Grand Stand.

At 221 for 7, Australia's requirement had risen to seven an over. Edwards contrived two more singles and was then out – sadly having to resort to a desperate swing, which gave an easy catch into the covers. His run accumulation was typical of the limited-overs game: 20 singles and two fours comprised his 28. Four balls later, Max Walker went for a run to Holder at backward square-leg, the new batsman Thomson sensibly sent him back, and Holder's throw hit the stumps. The *fourth* Australian run-out made the score 233 for 9 with only six overs and one ball left.

The West Indian crowd gathered at the boundary's edge, as Roberts came back for his last attack. His first ball to Thomson was quick and a full length; Thomson's downthrust was firm, and the ball rebounded past the fast bowler's feet, and on through to the straight boundary for four. It was the first time that Roberts (or Thomson) had been straight-driven to the boundary. In the same over Thomson got four more to square-leg. Lillee, facing Holder, now took four with a drive wide of the bowler. Thomson added a hectic two to long-leg and a dashed single. Four singles – two to each batsman – were raced in Roberts' next over. Some 20 runs had been added in the last three overs. Another 35 in four overs? Probably not, but the task no longer looked *impossible*.

In Holder's next over both batsmen ran like dervishes: three times they came back for a desperate second run after the ball had slid down towards fine-leg from bat or pad. With the throw on its way, some spectators began their charge in anticipation of another, final run-out: but Thomson's sprawling figure was adjudged not out, and sheepish West Indians were sent back from the field like errant schoolboys. Holder, who had bowled a no-ball earlier in this over, now bowled the seventh ball to Thomson. The bat heaved, the ball went weakly up in the air and Fredericks caught it at cover. This time those massed spectators came on like a tidal wave. They were almost at the wicket before it could be seen that umpire Tom Spencer's hand was again extended for a no-ball. With Fredericks throwing at, and past, the bowler's wicket, and spectators completely engulfing the scene, the opportunists Thomson and Lillee kept running between the wickets. The farce brought to mind stories of batsmen running forever with the ball lost in a tree, or buried by the heavy roller, or borne away on top of a London double-decker ...

... With the ball less than 30 yards away in the mêlée, the batsmen had run three – and Lillee was urging Thomson to keep going – when umpire Spencer called a halt. He walked over towards the official scorers in the Grand Stand, holding up two fingers. Or was it three? When that hectic over was finally finished all score sheets were not precisely in agreement as to what had happened. But they did agree with what was quite clear from the scoreboard, that 12 runs had been scored off the over and Australia were 268 for 9. Lillee and Thomson, looking serious and responsible, had added 35. They now needed 24 from the last three overs.

At 8.36 p.m., Roberts again. Two singles to Lillee, one to Thomson; and two balls beat the bat. Three only off the over meant 21 from the last two. The Possible had once again reverted to the Improbable.

Against Holder, Lillee took a single wide of mid-on. Thomson took a leg-bye. Lillee again an on-side single. But 10 an over needed more than this. Thomson swished at the fourth ball and missed, in exasperation started up the pitch for what would have been a crazy bye to the wicket-keeper, was sent back, and sprawled too late into his crease as Murray's underarm throw broke the wicket. A fifth run-out! The players raced for the pavilion while the Australian contingent remained, all of them, packed on the balcony taking photographs of the extraordinary scene.

The Duke of Edinburgh presented the Prudential Trophy to the winning captain who was, suitably, also Man of the Match. The longest day had produced a perfect cricket match: 565 runs between 11 a.m. and 8.42 p.m., and the West Indies winning cricket's first World Cup by 291 runs to 274.

N. H.